BREADCRUMBS

DAN MCKINNON

PRESS

This book is dedicated to my wife Donna, who had an absent husband during the times I spent writing these stories; thank you for letting me do this.

www.xulonpress.com

About *Breadcrumbs*

"Mark Twain once said, 'There was never yet an uninteresting life.' Most of us don't believe him. Dan McKinnon does. His sincerity in observing moments most miss allows him to see people most ignore. McKinnon's *Breadcrumbs* allows the reader to walk with him in noticing the mundane and unimportant that, in truth, are anything but mundane and unimportant."

—Chris Manginelli, Lead Pastor, Mill Creek Foursquare Church

Table of Contents

Breadcrumbs

A collection of stories by
Dan McKinnon

Acknowledgements

I want to acknowledge and thank the people who have helped me with this project, and those whose contributions to my life have been more global.

Thanks to my project coordinator at Xulon, Nick Lopez. You are patient and friendly. Thanks also to Toni Riggs, Publishing Consultant, with whom I initially spoke. Our spiritual conversation hooked me on Xulon.

Thanks to Brendan Gawlowski for your stellar editing. You took my humble writing to the next level, challenging and drawing me out, resulting in more clarity, focus, and creativity (and less wordiness; this parenthetical's for you!).

I've been receiving free legal advice from Phil Mattern for years; why should this project be different? Thanks for sticking with me, Phil. You are a good brother. I appreciate your gentle, sound, and godly counsel. It reminds me of James 3:17. (Look it up, people!)

Thank you to my wonderful family on my wife's side and my side.

Thanks to Calvin West for your friendship through the years.

Thanks to Jim and Pat Skrivseth for your love and support for many years.

I probably would not have made it to China without Paul Townsend's help. No China, no "Butterflies," to say nothing of the other ways he's encouraged and taught me over the years. Thanks for your support for my writing and freedom, Paul. I thank God for your enthusiasm for and support of the arts and culture, and for your zest for life.

Thanks to my good friend and prayer partner Ben Muzzey of Idaho. This book is full of you: cover and back-cover art, ideas, expressions, life, Jesus. You've read nearly everything I've written for 20 years, and always encouraged me. I probably would have given up without you. May your writings enjoy a broader readership after a while.

Thanks to my friend and pastor Chris Manginelli for pre-reading this material and your endorsement, and your leadership. You encouraged my writing long before this project. You are an inspiration; God has surely given you a good heart toward Him and people.

Introduction

In the Grimm fairy tale "Hansel and Gretel," Hansel leaves a trail of breadcrumbs for his sister and him to follow back home when their father takes them into the woods to abandon them. Although birds eat the breadcrumbs and thus nullify Hansel's wisdom, present-day website designers apply his strategy to online navigation and coined the term "breadcrumbs" or "breadcrumb trail" to denote a series of horizontal links on a webpage that a user can use to go back to previous pages, and all the way back to the landing or home page.

You hold in your hand or see on your screen a collection of short stories, memoirs, and vignettes that I wrote over a period of 15 years. You may wonder what they have in common. It is my hope that each, by God's grace, reveals a brief glimpse of the Most High, a breadcrumb if you will, that helped me see God in my circumstances. Little is much when God is in it. I hope these stories shine light on your path as well.

The poem "The Plan of the Master Weaver"[1] describes an analogy about the different ways God and humans view the events of people's lives. If we examine an embroidery from the back, we see a confusion of threads of different colors. Some threads hang short and knotted, others dangle in disarray. There is no apparent design, and this disorder is difficult to understand, much less appreciate. From the other side, one can see the tapestry's artistry displayed through the arrangement of pattern and color, its splendor inviting us to imagine the weaver.

Seeing the embroidery from the back is our perspective, and from the front, God's. He sees meaning in all the painful, difficult, and futile events and circumstances that define our lives. He knows that each thread is vital to the whole. In His kindness and by His power, He turns confusion to beauty, causing all things to work together for good for those who love Him, who are called according to His purpose.

We may never see the tapestry from the front as God does; we are finite beings. He generously allows us glimpses of it, however, and He gives us His spirit to view His marvelous workmanship with understanding and appreciation in a number of significant ways, whether by faith, His Word, or seeing things from His loving perspective.

There is another lens from which to view His involvement in human lives: retrospect. Looking back, we see a thread's beginning and track it through false starts, failures, disappointments, and sometimes trauma, to completion. These seemingly thwarted threads form His loveliest and most inspiring works, and have unlimited potential to help others. It is said that God does not greatly use a person whom He does not wound first. The most significant and unequalled of these injuries was to Jesus on the cross. His tortured death becomes our very life.

But in each life, some rain must fall, and in each person's life who receives it, there is a microcosm of that Great Cross. And as God did with Christ's passion and death, He makes everything in our lives meaningful and beautiful in its time. When life becomes desolate, painful, and confusing, even for an extended period of time, God is there, behind the scenes, working. He does not forget us.

God loves you and has a plan for you. Nothing you can imagine is as good as His plan. That message, however, links inexorably to this one: He may make you wait for what seems like a long time before His plan becomes evident in your life. I pray that as I reveal how God influenced my life, He will give you hope and even a glimpse of the gorgeous tapestry He is creating for *you*. Give Him time, trust and obey Him, and allow the things that He is doing in your life to play out. A day will come when all that you have prayed for happens, and that day may be tomorrow, or even today.

[1] Corrie ten Boom, a noted Christian author and speaker, quoted this poem in her speaking engagements, and it is sometimes attributed to her with the title "Life Is but a Weaving." However, others contend that Benjamin Malachi Franklin wrote it in the 1940s.

Butterflies

I was busy around the house while my wife visited her mother in a nearby city recently, and I used the relative calm to focus on my work. After a while, I took a break from searching for a job, and called my friend Ben, who lives in Idaho. I often feel better after talking with him, and have found I stress a bit less after we pray about our troubles. At the least, we have a sense that our worries have been placed in the hands of someone who can carry them.

I intended to call Ben using the landline because it was a better connection than my cell phone. I scrolled through the phonebook on the handset to find Ben's speed dial number, but I had to go by my dad's entry to get there.

Dad died a month earlier. I had called Ben since then, but had hurriedly moved past Dad's entry.

In the relative peace of the house, I sat there, looking at Dad's number, and figured the time had come to remove it. Unexpectedly, I began to cry. It had been the number of both my parents when Mom was alive, and became Dad's after her death in 2011. To me, that numeric combination was a part of my folks. Dad lived 1,100 miles away and I rarely talked to him without calling that number. These digits were randomly aligned decades ago, but their order had become so meaningful.

I realized that I could not call his numbers anymore, would never talk with him again, and I cried harder. I had called during good times and bad, when I needed something, when I wanted only to hear his voice, and, I suppose, to seek his approval, a need that stayed with me throughout my life. When he got sick a few years ago, I hoped my calls might cheer him up a bit, and at least distract him as he struggled to breathe with chronic obstructive pulmonary disease, a lung condition that slowly suffocated him to death.

Mom has been gone two years, and Dad only a month, but if I knew one thing, it was that life on Earth feels much different without parents. Consciously, I felt a void whenever I thought of them, but I believe the subconscious damage was more striking. My parents' presence and strength was with me my whole life; without it, I felt like an orphan. When I attained a goal, or saw something beautiful, or found something funny, I thought of them, and sometimes shared my feelings. I made sure to share what I thought might touch them or mean something special in their lives.

The position that God gave Dad as the father of his kids in this life was gone, except for memories. I was now the patriarch of my family. I realize this term has negative connotations for some in this culture, but whatever it might or might not mean or elicit, I now had that role. Everything was on me now, including matters I had some control over, and the things that I could only hope to influence. I would have to carry my Dad's generosity and affability while keeping the family together, trying to guide and advise those for whom I was responsible. There was a new family structure, and I had a great responsibility. This role weighed on my psyche, an old load freshly dropped on my shoulders. As I leaned on Dad, others now depended on me. I learned I had to seek God to help me bear this burden. Thank God there was that.

I remembered that, before removing Dad's numbers from the phone, before this grief, when I was nonetheless tired and burdened from other concerns, from my difficult day yesterday, lack of sleep last night, and work today, I looked out into the yard and saw a lovely white butterfly fluttering around the greenery in our vegetable garden. Whenever I saw a butterfly, I felt the palpable presence of God bringing me peace and comfort. It was a supernatural occurrence that happened each time I saw one, an event that began during seven very difficult weeks in China on a missionary trip. The gloomiest part of my suffering was the isolation I felt; despite being on a 17-person team, I did not have a friend to talk with, and phone calls to the States were expensive and rare. Through butterflies, I grew closer to Jesus, and I felt His comforting presence with me.

*   *   *

My rejections, missteps, and failures as I tried to go on a mission to China over a period of many years were mysterious to me until after I finally journeyed there, and God allowed me to see from time's vantage point how He worked all of these negatives together. I now have the sense that God allowed me to visit China when I was ready, and not a moment before.

How did God work in me, such that even glimpsing a common butterfly calms and centers me, stimulating my faith and allowing me to accept and see beyond my present difficulties? He did this in China, and it took me 12 years to arrive there and become immersed in a deeper pain that deconstructed the building blocks of my life to ground level, from which they could be rebuilt.

Years before I went to China, as someone just becoming acquainted with God, feeling Him drawing me, I attended a Presbyterian Church in Seattle's Capitol Hill neighborhood. One Sunday at church I found a pamphlet advertising an opportunity to work in China as a mechanic, fixing missionaries' cars. I had an aptitude and interest in automotive work, and China held an exotic appeal. But by and by, after I had raised my hopes, God closed this door, leaving me crushed and disappointed. I later saw that my motives for visiting were not pure, and that I didn't even know the God in whose name I would have gone. I thought it would have been enough that the missionaries whose cars I worked on knew Him.

Over the next seven years, I fully received the Lord and His spirit and began to serve Him in a small, predominantly African-American church as a choir member, pastor's aid committeeperson, and Sunday school teacher. I was learning about God amid difficulties at church: the poverty of our congregation, the challenges of recruiting congregants (or even getting the regulars to show up), and gaining credibility as a white man ministering in a predominantly black church. I also learned about God amid difficulties at my day job as a school bus driver, where I worked part-time on a split shift with no pay during the hours I was off in between. After five years, I left that church and began to attend a mostly white Pentecostal church, and during that time I made another significant effort to go to China as a missionary.

I occasionally visited my elderly friend's large Presbyterian Church in Seattle's University District, which had a department devoted to teaching English as a second language (also known as ESL programs). I saw a notice on the church bulletin board advertising that a missionary group would be traveling to China, and took one of the pamphlets. It was a two-month summer program, and I grew excited about going to China again. I had come a long way in my faith journey, and I became aware of how unready for the trip I had been earlier.

In preparation, I completed the ESL teacher's training course at the Presbyterian Church, and began teaching English to Ethiopian men.

When the missionary group's recruiter came to Seattle, I requested a meeting. I did not have a bachelor's degree, which the group required, though I had completed about 120 quarter hours of college across several disciplines. I also wanted to get married. These matters surfaced during the course of our talk, and the missionary representative gently suggested that I should contact him again after I married and earned my degree.

I mourned about this, but after some time let it go and forgot about China. A couple of years later, I married. We were happy and both working, my wife as a secretary and me as a City of Seattle transit bus operator (in common parlance, a bus driver). I had advanced from driving a school bus to a better paying job with good health benefits.

In a surprising turn of events a few years later, I unexpectedly had an inclination to take a community college course, and I signed up at a nearby school. I took two more classes the following quarter, one in English and the other in choir. At the end of the term, I applied to the University of Washington as a full-time undergraduate student.

I was so excited at the chance to be a full-time student, and I felt especially thrilled that returning to school didn't seem like my idea. Would God actually lead someone to go to college, and a secular school at that? It appeared that He did: with me! It stretched my belief that God could be so good, and so unorthodox. I completed my application and was happily surprised when the UW accepted me for fall quarter.

I had yet to decide upon a major. My great interest was in English literature and writing, but I finally chose an English major that prepared me to teach because I thought it would be a better career decision. There is, of course, the perennial joke that having an English degree of any kind prepares one to ask the question, "Would you like fries with that?" (There is at least one other, cruder joke about what one can do with the physical English degree diploma. Hint: the setting is a bathroom.)

I kept my part-time city bus-driving job. Each morning, I arose at four AM, worked until eight, and rushed over to school to catch my first class. I took as many as 18 credits per quarter, and combined with work and family responsibilities, I was one busy person.

I enjoyed college. I loved reading John Donne, Christopher Smart, and other notable Christian authors of early England, Dickens, Trollope, Austen, and the Brontes—Charlotte and Emily. Man, those early Britons had it goin' on. Many were believers. I saw a clear presentation of dynamic faith (as opposed to formal, stilted, and loveless) in *Jane Eyre*.

When I wrote papers, I did not hide my faith. By God's grace I did well academically, primarily because I prayed and was absorbed by the subject matter. Sometimes I went to Christian meetings instead of studying, and I requested prayer for all of my schoolwork, especially for papers and tests. In response to those prayers, I believe I was supernaturally gifted to do well. This may sound like an old wives' tale (an interesting expression, sexist *and* grammatically poor) but in my case, it wasn't a fable; there were times when my good grades could be attributed to no other cause than prayer. I did a fair amount of studying, but sometimes I felt like I was cheating in getting such good grades. Without fail, when I prayed beforehand, answers would come to me during tests, and my papers had structure and pizzazz that seemingly materialized as I wrote. I attained a 3.7 GPA, enough to graduate *cum laude* from the UW.

Driven by my sacrifices over the past two years as I worked and went to college, I voraciously coveted a well-paying job after school. At one job center, a recruiter thought I had strong enough credentials to apply at Microsoft. What she said thrilled me, but I didn't apply at the time, figuring I would surely do so after graduation. But a funny thing happened on my way to the forum: God showed up.

As graduation approached, a feeling that I was to go to China after graduation grew inside of me. Initially, I was dubious and surprised. I was now 40, and hadn't thought about going to China for five years. I had simply forgotten about it, and I assumed that God had also, or He would have opened a door for me to go earlier, when I wanted to so badly. I had changed, and had other priorities now.

I can't explain how I could tell God now wanted me to go to China. I just knew that He was reminding me of my former zeal to go. He wanted me to prepare. I realized that I would have my degree in a few weeks, and that I had been married three years, both of the goals the recruiter said I should achieve before contacting him again.

I soon contacted English Language Institute China (ELIC), the group I came across through the Presbyterian Church years before. They sent me information about their summer program, which was still open for that year. I learned that I would have to raise $2,300 of support for the trip. I had almost that much in the bank and figured that raising money was the least of my worries. If I couldn't raise the support, I'd just pay my own way.

I then began to compose a list of people to whom I could send support letters. I included family, friends, and people from my church. I distributed the letters and waited. I sent these out because ELIC's instructions said I should, rather than from financial need. The recruiter said it would make for better prayer support. Though the response to my letters was underwhelming, I was unconcerned because I could pay my own way. God had something else in mind, however.

At the time, my wife and I drove a nifty little Buick Skylark that we liked and entirely depended on for transportation. The transmission broke, and it cost $1,700 to fix. That and other expenses quickly erased all of our savings. Surprisingly, God did not allow those events to entice others into donating more money for my trip; the support simply did not appear.

After weeks of this financial paralysis, I had grown angry with God. After working so hard to get my degree, I had put my dreams of a good-paying job on hold—to say nothing of my current job and life—to go to China. I was even going without my wife, as she did not have a bachelor's degree. I had only a matter of weeks to raise a substantial portion of my funds. God had allowed my savings to disappear, and now there was no plan B. He didn't seem to be aware of the problem. His silence felt like neglect.

My good friend Paul organized a support gathering with food and Christian music. It was a merry and pro-ductive gathering, and God encouraged all attendees. It raised some money toward my goal, though not nearly enough. (Later, I recognized that Paul's faith, love, belief in me, and willingness to do practical things with our community to help me provided vital moral support.)

I had applied for a leave of absence from work to go to China. One morning after my route, the base chief, an African-American woman, called me into her office to discuss my leave. She asked why I needed time off, and I informed her that I would be teaching English in China. In a moment of boldness, I told her that I was a Christian and the purpose behind our group's trip was to evangelize through our service as English teachers and directly through informal one-on-one and small-group interactions with our students. She began to weep. She said God was telling her to give me $500 toward my support. I had never met or even laid eyes on her before that morning.

More financial support trickled in, but slowly. Though I carried on, I remained miffed at God and confused by His ways. The time of departure drew near. We were to meet in Los Angeles at a Christian college for a week of training before leaving for China. I was under great pressure because I had to decide what to do within three days: go without all of my support, or cancel my journey and admit that I hadn't heard God. I would have had to return the money that I had already received. Worse, I'm not sure my faith would have ever recovered after all the work I had gone through to prepare for the trip. I gritted my teeth, and used some of the support money to buy an airline ticket for Los Angeles. I was about $500 short of $2,300. I committed, but I wasn't happy.

After a few days of training in Los Angeles, the rest of my support came in. Before I left, a surplus had accumulated in my account, and I was able to give money to teachers who did not have enough. As my former African-American pastor used to say, "Look at God!"

Joy comes after trials.

*   *   *

I taught English to adult, native-Chinese English teachers at Hunan Institute of Education in a city named Changsha in Hunan province. They arrived at campus from all over the region, released from their duties of teaching English to students of various ages for seven weeks. Our missionary group had a contract with the Chinese government to instruct English teachers only, but we suspected that there were "plants" among our students who were not actually teachers, and who were improving their English primarily for commercial or political reasons. In my class, I had a math professor who specialized in fuzzy logic. He had trouble hiding his brilliance. He invited me to his house one Sunday afternoon for lunch with his wife and daughter. He told me that he had given presentations on mathematics in Europe and that he urgently needed to improve his English. One "teacher" was apparently an electronics executive, another, a sales representative of some sort.

The college where we'd been assigned to teach was an aged, Russian-built brick schoolhouse with huge, glassless eight-foot windows. The building was emblematic of a forgotten era when the Union of Soviet Socialist Republics, by its largesse and ambitious oversight, mentored China toward similar ideological goals, though it had only been a Marxist nation itself for 27 years.

Intensely hot air wafted through the big windows into our classroom from the primitive college courtyard. I bathed in lukewarm water in an old tub in my room every day before trudging to class (there was no shower) and by 10 AM, laboring on my feet in front of my 21 adult students, I sweated so profusely that it looked like I had just gone swimming fully clothed in the Xiang River. (I never swam in the Xiang, though the blazing heat of the region sorely tempted me. School officials warned us that under no circumstances were we to swim in the muddy channel, and at the beginning of our stay, someone reported seeing a dead human body float sluggishly downstream.)

Light-headed, anxious, and weak, I beat the placid air in front of my class, struggling to instill proper English into my overtired, overheated students. Though interested, they were often dazed and distracted. They seemed to like me, though I supposed they would have liked Paris Hilton if she were standing before them, so I couldn't take much comfort from their sentiment. Overall they were optimistic and sympathetic; some held the slight hope that their presence here would magically enhance their future lives. For others, it was at least a break from their routine. One student, however, hated the United States, and insulted America and Americans at every opportunity, especially the one Providence had placed conveniently in front of him.

I sought to convey the subtle aspects of English and I realized that much of what I took for granted with my native tongue was difficult to articulate, particularly given their limited vocabularies and inexperience with English. (This stuff seemed second nature to me, but then I'd had 40 years of practice in an English-speaking country.) My apprentices, though willing, struggled.

One day, I was startled by a withering audible assault. Through the room's giant, open casement, I observed a Chinese MiG rip through the sweltering haze behind the Chinese Communist flag, bright yellow stars on a field of brilliant red, fluttering in the empty school courtyard. That I had just seen a strange sight was apparent, though my class barely reacted. It dawned on me that although my response to this environment was genuine, I was also an alien.

*   *   *

I was a stranger in a remarkably strange land. I often felt misplaced in the States, for that matter, but this was even more pronounced. Since the beginning of recorded history, the people here had been incubated in a system so different from the Western world.

There was precious little air-conditioning in China. Temperature was measured in Celsius, and as I never knew exactly how hot it was, this disorientation added to my discomfort. I wanted precise Fahrenheit documentation for my bearings, and to earn sympathy from relatives and friends stateside. I suppose I was accumulating spiritual capital for my return home as the suffering overseas missionary.

I smelled. Asian bacteria sprang into action minutes after bathing and donning clean clothes. Our teaching schedule was rigorous, and during "off duty" time we were supposed to interact with our students, taking opportunities afforded by leisure activities to teach English beyond the classroom, to "make it real." The primary organized way we did this was to portray American life through primitive plays depicting historical US events and modern cultural vignettes. In one of the former,

I played Abraham Lincoln with a white cotton beard (I'd never seen Lincoln with a white beard) and a paper stovepipe hat constructed from white paper sketchily colored with black crayon. In turn, we watched as our hosts enacted various dramas about their country in English. The plays required preparation and effort and were designed to present opportunities for teaching and learning. They also seemed to be a subtle celebration of American cultural superiority; it was unclear whether it was the Chinese, Americans, or both promoting this, but sometimes these events resulted in a dull and oppressive anxiety for me. In addition to the plays, we often went for walks with students, visited their austere quarters, shared meals, and spent time together in an effort to unearth even more teaching opportunities (a crossword puzzler might say "teach-ops").

I was assigned an assistant teacher, a Chinese national named Wong, who was about 10 years my junior. One midsummer morning, Wong and I had a day off from our teaching duties, and he took me downtown. We hoped for a relaxing break from our strenuous schedules, focused teammates, and our at-times demanding students. We boarded a bus that was about the size of a Seattle coach, but of Slavic make, grubby and tired. The retractors that connected the overhead poles to electric wires were droopy, filthy hemp instead of clean, taut metal cable. We boarded near the beginning of the route. Seats were plentiful, the windows open, and the air circulated in the bus interior as the coach meandered along its route on the crowded thoroughfare toward the core of the city.

People streamed aboard the old coach at each stop until it was overfull and uncomfortable, as if this were the only inbound vehicle to the metropolis that day. I wanted to yell, "Stop letting people on!" to the coach operator, but of course I didn't. The driver mechanically continued his cycle: stop, open the sluice gate to waves of humanity, close and repeat, a sorcerer's apprentice with no strength or will to resist newcomers or advocate for his crushed passengers.

In the United States, litigation *may* often be frivolous, but it also protects people from being trampled on public transport. When a bus is full in Seattle, drivers call in to request another coach. Full buses move past stops with waiting passengers, who must then wait for backup buses. Perhaps China's civil agencies need to be prosecuted a couple of times for the public good, though something tells me that this is not going to happen.

The overcrowding on board became almost comical, a significant disconnect between the driver's state of mind and that of his passengers. One young woman perspired freely as she stood near me, holding a baby. Her obvious fatigue and the blank look in her eyes alarmed me. Was she losing consciousness? Overcome momentarily by compassion, and probably a yen to instruct the Chinese in ways of Western righteousness, I gave her my seat. Wong, younger, more energetic, and in better health than I but also used to the ways of China, retained his. Mildly shaking his head in puzzlement, he shot me a funny look, pondering this unusual American. On some level he was responsible for me; he never flagged in treating me with respect, but may have also thought me a fool.

The novelty of the lark downtown and attendant feelings left me, replaced by intense concern. I was now standing unprotected from the waves of people who pushed against me. An attractive Asian woman seemed to enjoy our close quarters, and pressed against me. As a married man, I felt guilty for not resisting.

On the day of our bus ride, the outside temperature reached 90°, and inside the crowded bus perhaps topped 100°. Droplets of perspiration appeared on my face and neck, dripping lazily, gaining mass, and soaking my shirt and pants, their easy slide neatly mocking my predicament. Trapped, panicky, and lightheaded, I thankfully did not lose consciousness. After a few moments of acute anxiety, passengers gradually began slipping out of the bus, and the issue receded, serving as just one more ordeal God took me through in China. Next! Take a number!

By this time, I'd been in Changsha for several weeks. I didn't have the strength or willpower to actively hate the sticky heat, my strained relationships with hosts and teammates, our overzealous work schedule, or any number of other things that might torque me stateside. Like a ball in the devil's pinball machine, I caromed from one awful trial to another. I *was* often perplexed by the hidden, unpredictable, authoritarian power structure that dominated me and others in China, though I was not— and thanked God for it—a citizen of the People's Republic of China. I often felt sorry for Wong, the other assistant teachers, and my students, who bore this oppression daily with very little realistic hope of relief, ever. Government officials had ordered Wong to be my assistant in a city several hundred kilometers away from his wife for two months, and he had no choice but to comply.

Between a robust work schedule and a strange diet that affected me like poison, I lived a feeble, humbling, moment-to-moment existence. Unfortunately for Christians, this weakened state is just where the Lord wants us. When we are weak, we bear fruit because the people we hope to influence for the gospel don't hate or fear us so much, and they lower their guard. Our frailty undermines their suspicion. The *lingua franca* between humans is anguish. Troubled souls converse fluently, though often wordlessly, even if they bear different religious labels.

No one speaks from a deeper place than Jesus. He converses with anyone, and those who suffer deeply hear and trust Him without difficulty. His dilemma is that His servants don't take naturally to suffering with Him. Being kind, He doesn't want to disown them, but how will His wondrous, necessary work of comforting the afflicted be accomplished? The Good Book says that if we are to reign with Him, we must also suffer with Him.

I spoke only a little Chinese, but even among Chinese people who spoke English, I had trouble understanding what was going on culturally, politically, and interpersonally. This spectacularly unfamiliar environment hosted insidious microorganisms that enjoyed toying with North Americans. We weren't exactly eating the kind of Chinese food found in American restaurants, either. Although our hosts provided the best food they had, it did not agree with me, especially the abundant use of oil (which the Chinese considered a luxury). Eventually I could take only rice, and in two months, my weight dropped from 155 to 128 pounds. I felt it most when I was in bed, my bony legs resting against each other as I lay on my side, my hip chiseling into the thin, hard mattress.

At long last and after much suffering, our summer session ended. We were rewarded by a trip from Changsha to Beijing, travelling by rail, as most Chinese did. The trip lasted 16 hours. Through a thick haze, I saw the dim ochre Chinese sunset beyond the rice paddies and Soviet industrial buildings built in a bygone era. The smog skewed everything and was reminiscent of the gauzy look in old Hollywood films that was created by putting gel on the camera lens, but this was no picture or movie. It was real and the scene created a profound impression. I was not sure how many Americans have seen or ever will see this, the land pristine in that sense. As I watched the colors of the subdued Asian palette and the peculiar forms of the land and people, music seemed to resonate from bamboo flutes and bowed fiddles, somehow played by the spirits of the people, of their republic of China, a sound that fit its surroundings perfectly but was foreign to my Western sensibilities.

The environment was fundamentally different from North America. I was disoriented and fully immersed in exotic sensations that evoked an emotional response I seemed incapable of producing. It was also hard to articulate, "mind-bending" beyond the drug-influenced connotations of a hippie vocabulary. As I watched the countryside sweep by, I considered the idea that the "Communist" in "Communist China" might feel like an add-on, that there was something here before 1926 (the start of the civil war that toppled the government in 1949) that was intrinsically Chinese and unchangeable by ideology. Though grafted deeply by pain, starvation, and warfare, communism was a political solution, but also possibly an addition. China now is the China of long ago.

*   *   *

Going to China that summer was the most challenging thing I had done to that point in my life. My weight loss was alarming, and I carried an almost continual feeling of nausea and weakness while there. Sick, frail, and often exhausted, I never managed to sleep longer than four hours in a night. Upon returning, I discussed my insomnia with a Christian medical doctor. The physician told me that he struggled with sleep as acutely as I had when he was on the mission field. There was some relief and confirmation in that.

In my moments in China when I didn't think I could take any more, God arranged for a butterfly to appear for a few moments in a way that I could not miss. It happened so regularly, at the hardest times of my stay, that I saw a pattern in it and recognized God. It was obvious that He had placed it there just for me: "I have not left you. I am with you. You can make it. Hold on."

Today, when I see a butterfly, I don't have to consciously remember what God did for me in China. I automatically, physically feel God's touch, which lifts me above my circumstances into His presence and peace. This miracle alone was worth the trip. It is my hope that He also used me in spite of myself to show His love to others.

*   *   *

I saw a butterfly before I removed Dad's numbers from my phone. I also have a hope that I will speak to him again on the other side.

Short story

Chief

I am a Blackfoot Indian, the son of a chief. Some in my tribe treat me like a chief. But things are different now. Reservation life weakens chiefs.

I talk today about the white men who tried to kill me. About why I helped them after they tortured me.

Last week wasn't the first time they made trouble for me. They don't like me. They don't like me because they don't like Indians. I never hurt them but they don't like me anyway.

I was out in the wilderness. I heard them coming from a long way off. I could have avoided them easily but I wanted to trade. Thoughts of a good trade made me forget that they don't like Indians.

They were drinking. They wanted to make me drink, like I used to. But I don't drink any more. The Great Spirit took it from me. The Great Spirit gave my life back to me. The Great Spirit showed me that Indians are wondrous people, and that drink destroys them.

They were angry when I wouldn't drink. They poured beer on me. They beat me. Then they tied me up. They urinated on me. I watched as they did each of these things. I couldn't stop them.

They stole my canteen and sup≠plies. They left me to die. I couldn't get loose or move. In a dream, I saw how to get free.

Two days later I saw a dust cloud rising across the valley, above the old mine. When I got close, I saw that the mine had collapsed. It had fallen on them.

They drank more after they left me. They drank whiskey and beer. Then they went into the mine. They were drunk and used one of the posts for target practice. The one named Frank used his shotgun. The post broke and the mine caved in.

It took me a long time to dig into the mine. I moved rocks and dug as fast as I could. I heard a noise coming from behind a rock. Men were trapped behind that rock.

I left the mine and hurried to town. I moved fast but it took a whole day. I told the sheriff about the trapped men. He and some others went and freed the men from the mine. Frank and another man died. Three others survived.

You want to know why I went to town to get help for the men after what they did to me.

Two years ago, white missionaries came to our reservation. They were strange people, stranger than other whites. They had a message for us. I could see a difference between them and the message they carried. But I saw that their message was true. That the Jesus they talked about was the son of the Great Spirit. It was easy to see because the Spirit made it easy for me to see. I saw it right away. I knew it was true even if those missionaries were strange. I guess they couldn't help being strange.

Jesus said do good to your enemies. He told me to help the men. This was not how I was raised. I didn't like the men who treated me bad. I had to forget about that. I just had to think about what Jesus wanted me to do.

I don't hate the men who survived. They look at me different now. Maybe if they drink, they would do the same thing again. I don't know. It doesn't make any difference. I would do the same thing again. That is what Jesus wants.

Three Days and Counting

S mit was past demerits now, and into serious trouble. Just *one day* No Response (NR) warranted a heavy fine, and a triple penalty was levied if one remained off the grid for a second day. Beyond that a *planet resident* was banished to the Bin to do hard time indefinitely.

*   *   *

Banglidore Shaw, *Sanjat* of the Recursive Realm, was stressed because responsibility for AWOL citizens like Smit rested heavily upon him. He did take comfort in comparing his anxiety with what Smit would experience when they found him. And find him they would. No one, not even all-tier processing geniuses who could outthink machines, managed to stay lost for long, and this man was mid-tier at best.

Shaw sighed at the thought of machines getting exclusive credit for his department's impeccable record of finding all NRs. Computers were nothing without talented programmers.

But just as a smart countermove in chess can unravel a brilliant attack, another thought intruded into the *Sanjat's* mind: Computers had long had the ability to write pristine, human-logic programs themselves. Sometime soon, perhaps even now, newly constructed computers would think freely, capable of *inferencing* like the drone fishing boats that were set at liberty to ply the seas, gathering fish for *planet residents*. Shaw suppressed a qualm in his gut as he considered that such intelligent instruments might eventually be granted dominion over humans.

Smit, like everyone else, wore a Locator, but certain elites could legally turn theirs off, and a few clever criminals knew how to disable the device. The defector was in the latter category of non-locatables.

The concept for the Locator originated as an outgrowth of the cellular phone, a development that occurred long before Shaw was born. "One person, one number," had been the marketing slogan of Horizon, the dominant cell phone pusher for as long as anyone could remember, eventually to be absorbed by the Recursive Realm government. (Or had Horizon absorbed the government?) Soon after, *point probers*, humans whose only job was to look for patterns in data, realized that an individual's area code, prefix, and suffix phone number (also known as one's Number Horizon) was curiously similar to their social security number, a simple and profound revelation that had eluded many. Generations ago the federal government, spurred in part by relentless lobbying from wealthy cell phone companies like

Horizon, yielded power and became their silent partner, like a titular monarch over numerous, potent ministers. The company and the Fed married, powerfully aligning as a government-industrial complex, with little distinction between their spheres of influence. Cell phone companies essentially transferred each citizen's social security number to their phone, combining one's social security number, calling number, and location index.

The *Sanjat* marveled that anyone had ever paid for a cell phone. For as long as he could remember, a citizen's right and responsibility to vote was contingent on their acceptance and legal use of a cell phone. Shaw found the restrictions easy enough to comply with: all he had to do was avoid tampering with its software or hardware, register the phone for yearly software upgrades, and answer it every time a certified A-grade machine or person called, summoned, or vibrated. (The deaf received their messages visually or by pulse, the blind via changeable Braille pad.) Shaw, like all citizens, was required to respond to A-grade communiqués within 24 hours. He saw that, per protocol, Smit had been sent such a message after his first day NR; six hours had passed since.

*   *   *

Smit gave his surroundings a casual glance as he staggered toward the diner. He couldn't go on any longer without food. He had long since run out of credits, and even if he had any, swiping his hand through the scanner now would alert careTakers; they would have him within the hour. Even if he somehow escaped, the telltale scanner would reveal his location within a kilometer, which was much more than they knew now. In his current state, he couldn't move quickly. Famished and exhausted, he opened the door to the restaurant.

With the evening rush a few hours away, the restaurant was not crowded. Still, Smit had to sit at the counter because each small table had occupants, though just one or two. People were like that; they didn't mix voluntarily. He was ravenous now, filled with a hunger gnawing at the caution he knew he must exercise to stay free. He wasn't going to eat next to anyone. It was an unnecessary risk, a gamble that would surely haunt him later.

As he sat down, a drone said "good evening," and told him to take his time selecting the eatables he desired. Instead of using the drone to order, Smit depressed the button on its side, alerting the only wait-person in the diner, who didn't appear happy to have to serve someone.

"So what's the matter with you?" the pimply adolescent asked. Smit gestured at his throat with his hand and shook his head. "You don't even have enough for a voice transplant," the waiter mumbled disconsolately, any hope for a tip draining from him.

Not only will you not get a tip, your boss will take a loss on anything I eat here tonight, thought Smit. Feigning that he couldn't speak was risky because it drew attention, but he worried that if he allowed the drone to take his order, as was custom, it would send a sample of his voice to be compared to criminals on file. Smit pointed to the menu items he desired, unconcerned about price. He had bunched a big towel under his overcoat to simulate portliness, hoping this would imply that he'd done without a voice transplant in order to have more money to eat.

After devouring a big breakfast of egg-o-like, simu-bac meat product, flapjack substitute, and a flagon of coff-eine, Smit reconnoitered to clear his escape. After the waiter passed through the swinging doors to the kitchen, Smit fled the diner.

*   *   *

The *Sanjat* spent most of his time at the NRC waiting. He had various projects to attend to, but the criminals he tracked had to make a mistake before he could catch them. Smit was proving to be more elusive than most.

A nagging, previously suppressed thought crept into Shaw's subconscious, a subtle feeling that something was wrong. It pertained to the system he administered. It was true that he was not very high in the administration's hierarchy, but he spent his considerable talents and abundant energy perpetuating the *avant-status-quo*, a term made popular by the current Premier. It meant that the present system, the code in its grandeur, was static and dynamic simultaneously, and that the dynamic facet was progressive. This static/dynamic quality was only one way in which the code was paradoxical. It was also, while stable and immutable, adaptable. Interestingly, this flexibility indistinctly linked to the Premier. As Shaw considered the intellectual intricacies of the code, he knew that if someone did not side with the Premier, she or he would not advance very far in the hierarchy of the Realm. Such a person might even face prosecution.

Shaw knew that his clearest thinking came to him like this, at an almost subliminal level as his whole being processed a problem rather than his cognitive mind alone. Answers to complex puzzles came to him while asleep or upon awakening, when thinking about the problem or while performing mundane tasks. He had always possessed this gift. It opened doors for him, helped him advance to his present position at the NRC.

But there was something about this new non-locatable, the whole spirit associated with him and this caper, that worried him and aroused his suspicions.

*   *   *

Sometime during President O'Houlihan's reign, Congress passed an unusual bill that expanded democracy considerably beyond the inadequate notions of the Constitution's framers. For some time now, planet residents *voted electronically each day, on every law, position, and governmental action. Sometimes voters relegated their power of choice to their representatives, especially on lesser issues.*

Citizens participated wholeheartedly in important matters, but even in this arena, they leaned upon their representatives for reliable information. Representatives in turn depended on Data Assayers, who were tasked with evaluating information and purging impurities. Data Assayers were appointed and funded by the office of the Premier.

*   *   *

What if the Premier had hidden motives? It was a risky thought, one Shaw would not be able to share. The voters granted the Premier his power, but their perception of him or her was fully dependent on the verity of their information. Of course, the Premier had influence over that information, but nobody seemed to know how much.

And what of this Smit? Shaw booted up the Mercator, a dated machine that he despised. He appreciated devices that did not stumble with big programs. He had grown up in Bangalore, where he and his peers were taught computing as they learned to walk and speak. The Mercator was a carry-over from a previous era, but it would have to suffice for this.

He began to converse with the machine in MS-MOL, a dated but relatively effective collection of machine object language instructions and parameters. The old machine's clicks and hums echoed dully off the synthetic, inadequately soundproofed walls of his dot-gov office.

"Subject: Non-locatables.

"Param: (Smit).

"Param: (to the present time).

"Param: (bio)."

Smit's numeric location index flashed in the Mercator's holograph momentarily while the old box retrieved the missing man's complex file. Shaw called an arbitrary bookmark and the machine responded in the quick, sing-song ramble of hyperspeech: "Subject Smit had trouble in his mid-thirties. Unspecified informant at one of Smit's occupation-callings reported Smit for non-tangential spiritual beliefs."

This is out of the ordinary. The code required a person to follow a spiritual path that harmonized with the many roads to perfection. Smit's apparently had not.

It was also unsettling. Shaw had always suspected—known, really—that there was only one higher power. But that belief was repugnant to the present powers and culture.

*   *   *

Smit ran until he could run no more, until even the terror of capture couldn't spur him on. He collapsed clumsily onto the pedestrian corridor, and rolled until his back rested against the monolithic barrier surrounding a government-mercantile structure. The computerized fence quickly warned him to remove himself, quoting code. He did so slowly, half-heartedly.

In great anguish, he vomited. His heart sank. All of the effort and strategizing, working with the fear, had been for nothing. He condemned himself for giving in to his hunger, overriding the truth that he simply had to eat. He had satisfied his desire, and there it was on the corridor, smelly and revolting, not associable to the victuals he had so eagerly consumed.

The sensors in the corridor alerted the resident CPU. "Remove your matter from the corridor or I will summon careTakers," a woman said unemotionally. Those warned by this message were certainly motivated by her reference to the aforementioned party, not from her voice inflection. Smit feared them, but he was too tired to move.

Smit lay on his back on the smooth surface of the pedestrian corridor, unblemished except for his throw-up. He looked into heaven. He wanted a last look before being thrown into the hell of the Bin.

*   *   *

Maybe it was the jazz, thought the *Sanjat*, some musical taint that had spoiled Smit's life. Smit loved jazz, and played clarinet in the style of an *avant* Benny Goodman. On a whim Shaw called in quick succession, "Subject: Man.

"Param: (Benjamin Goodman).

"Param: (bandleader/clarinetist).

"Param: (selection). Execute selection."

As the beat and melody of the song swung through the dingy office, Shaw recalled what he'd learned about jazz. He knew he couldn't fully appreciate a jazz tune without learning the original composition. Then one could better understand the improvisational nature of the art. Songs were usually ballads or commercially successful standards, which musicians and singers played, creating new melodies to the same chord structure. This had little meaning to Shaw. With time, though, he thought he might cultivate a real appreciation for this art form because he could feel it. The rhythm compelled him to move his body in time to the music emanating from the Mercator.

More puzzling to Shaw was how this music could bring a person to a place of non-tangential beliefs. The music and those who created it enjoyed a freedom present in other arts, and perhaps even to a greater degree. A thought dawned upon him reminiscent of other inspirations he'd had. Maybe an association with another player had tainted Smit.

Surely that's it. Shaw looked up some of the other players with whom Smit played in those days. They all took similar attitudes toward the code and many pretended there was no system, playing all night and creating their own space, much like Virtual Reality players did in cyberspace. When the code had come, SysAdmins tried to bend all life, including Art, Media, and Cyberspace, into its rigidity. There had been a backlash from groups like these musicians. They tried to create their own world through music, an effort to escape the rigidity of their lives under the code.

*   *   *

Partly as a way to overcome and absorb the backlash from artists and musicians, the code had needed to become more flexible. Programming was intrinsically inflexible until Artificial Intelligence (AI) grew more sophisticated and comprehensive. The Assemblor considered these changes "huge." (She wasn't one of the Sanjat's *favorite people, but that was immaterial, and his problem.)*

AI changed things. Previously, a computer could perform only what it was programmed to do. But with nearly infinite looping, fuzzy logic, and holistic algorithms, machines developed the ability to choose and learn. They learned to discern the best choice among infinite possibilities, subject to guiding priorities defined by the Assemblor and her close team of select programmers.

*   *   *

The *Sanjat* recognized that the code was analogous to spiritual paths. At least this was the party line, unquestioned since he had first been tested in his youth. The code decreed that the topmost priority was a god, the agreed-upon God, and machines' and people's paths to it multitudinous; therein lay uniformity of purpose and goal. Was this not true freedom?

The warm jazz ceased and the cold hyperspeech of the Mercator broke unpleasantly into Shaw's reveries: "Entering standby mode…"

"So go already!" Shaw yelled. He wanted to throw something at the machine, break it apart and destroy its core. But he didn't. He had work to do.

And then Shaw had a funny thought. *What would it be like to work in this office with jazz playing in the background?*

*   *   *

Four careTakers—though one would have sufficed—unceremoniously deposited Smit at the gate, making a token effort not to hurt him, as programmed. Several gateKeepers operated the complex security measures on the door to open it safely. A few newMins later, they shoved Smit through the portal, casting him among the leprous and lost tenants of the underworld. Revulsion wrenched his intestines as he panted quick, shallow gasps, and tried to stay away from the freaks and get back to his former, familiar realm.

*   *   *

Many of the people in the Bin were fryOuts, bearers of a puzzling mental illness that had started concurrently with O'Houlihan's reign. O'Houlihan served two terms as president. His vice president, Hal Boor, then started a presidential term with O'Houlihan as his vice president, until Boor's AI circuits crashed for good. O'Houlihan ascended to the presidency once more, not to descend until his death twenty years later, the victim of an incurable sexually transmitted disease. Apocryphal historians later claimed that O'Houlihan had arranged Boor's downfall, in the world's first electronic coup d'etat.

*   *   *

Shaw read the latest report with interest. Smit had been captured. The gateKeepers had already passed him through the gate. He was in the Bin.

Shaw was surprised how disappointing this news was to him. When he first received Smit's case—without even knowing the man—he assumed Smit was arrogant and hateful, the perfect enemy of *planet residents* whom Shaw, as *Sanjat,* was to serve and protect.

An admiration for Smit surfaced in the *Sanjat's* consciousness. It had been there all along, a vague feeling that he suppressed whenever it gained mass or clarity. What was it like to be Smit? What was it like to play jazz like that? What did he feel when doing it?

Shaw knew that he had been gifted, he supposed by God, to have revelations that accelerated his processes, advanced the work on his deliverables, and even gave him wings to new career heights. These ideas were where his real talent had its roots, and his natural abilities took over from there. It was tempting to flout this gift over others and to let his abilities puff out his ego, or if he controlled them, to at least elevate his own opinion of himself to a dangerous level. He knew of Data Assayers who had done that.

But the thing itself, the revelations and his innate thinking ability to recognize and synthesize them—apart from any pride or arrogance it might, or might not, create in him or others—was the real thing. Talent. Ability. Freedom. Was this what Smit felt as he played jazz? Was this what Shaw saw in himself?

*   *   *

FryOuts could no longer reason. In the early years of the first Web, sweeping technological developments chaotically reordered syntactical standards, and certain programmers simply tried to learn too much too quickly. Some had not begun programming early enough in their lives, as Shaw and his peers had, and had burned out, the first victims of data deluge. It was as if their desperate need for more storage space in their brains and their appetite to learn had cannibalized their fundamental reasoning processes. Later, Techists devised ways to link native human reasoning to manufactured bio-databases. The first subjects of this technology did not fare well. Years later the brain's communication channels broke down, similar to the way that the human body used to reject donor organs or breast implants. The foolishness of trying to turn the human mind into a file server dawned in the collective human consciousness. But how else could they address this need?

Creating effective schema and formulating the Meta categories for databases was incredibly complex, and strained the human mind nearly as much as remembering all that mundane data, as previous programmers nearly did inadvertently. The guiding priorities that modern machines needed to write code required more brainpower than any human could supply. Machines kept offering their assistance, and men continued punting their problems to the computers. Politicians proposed new legislation, allowing machines to bear the brunt of the load. Things were under control at present because machines did all the coding. Few knew if they were audited effectively, if the machines had secrets. Who really knew except God?

*   *   *

Shaw tried to imagine Smit in his present circumstances, among the castoffs of the present age. No one knew what it was like to live there. There was simply no communication. Furthermore, no one wanted to know. Generations ago it had been legal to communicate with and even visit prisoners. Even then no one did. Now it was neither legal nor possible.

*   *   *

Smit awoke suddenly and immediately knew where he was: the Bin. He remembered how he had gotten here. He was among the fryOuts and others. He checked his feelings and realized he didn't care. He was too tired to be afraid, relieved that his ordeal was over. Still, rumors Smit had heard about the Bin made him vaguely uneasy. Was the mental illness this place was infamous for contagious? What could he expect?

*   *   *

The *Sanjat* knew a secret. He had some dirt on the present Assemblor.

Surreptitiously, he'd installed one of his sniffer programs on her workstation (no small feat) and it noted the exact time she inserted her Random Access Index into the program. Certain criminal Assemblors used this practice to guarantee their longevity, and Shaw could prove the present Assemblor was guilty of it. A Data Assayer had verified his sniffer's data, without bothering to note the content. This was very handy for Shaw, though the offense might get the Data Assayer fired, especially considering that the intelligence in this case pertained to the Assemblor. Fired Data Assayers never worked again and most eventually found themselves in the Bin after years of rejection by society. Data Assayers were celebrities, and even still, some ended up in the Bin. It was a marvel. Their importance became a drug that exposed their character weaknesses, making them careless.

Shaw knew that this kind of data could be manufactured, but it was prohibitively expensive; if the case did go to trial, Shaw's poverty would be an advantage when the jury software interrogated him.

What he had was probably not huge, but it indicated something suspicious about the Assemblor. How big it turned out to be depended on her fear.

*   *   *

Smit wandered among the dead. They stared at him vacantly. Some drew figures in the dirt with sticks or their fingers. He tried to read one and saw it was newParadigm Machine Language, very advanced, but linked to nothing concrete, a mildly interesting study in impracticality, signifying nothing.

He saw some individuals moving with purpose among the fryOuts. These ministered to the prisoners' needs, giving them food, helping them. He approached one of the ministers, a woman with long black hair, dressed in rags.

"Who are you, and why do you help these people?" Smit asked the woman.

"The Master is well pleased when we help them," she said with a smile so pure he couldn't recall seeing the like.

"But where do you get this food? And who is the Master?"

"We grow it, over there," she said, pointing to a valley beyond a turn in the one road leading away from the gate. She didn't answer his second question.

"Is the Master here?"

"In spirit," she said. "It is enough. His teachings spring from two foundations: Love God, and love others as yourself." With that, she resumed her ministrations to the gentle residents of this strange valley.

*   *   *

"I want to go through the gate!" the *Sanjat* demanded of the angry Assemblor. She watched him through expressionless eyes. She could have summoned careTakers, but he was wily: *What was his aim?*

"You know that is against the code. It is foolish of you to mention it and beneath the dignity of your intellect. Why should I allow it?"

"Because I know and can prove you entered your Random Access Index into the program."

Ah. She restrained her anger, forcing her face into a tranquil mask. She learned to do this in school years ago, one among many chosen at birth to attend the prestigious Serpentine School. At that time she had had power only in her fantasies, scheming far into the night while her peers slept. She needed less sleep because of the drug *somnegate*, a discovery that actually enabled a person to receive the benefits of sleep while they were conscious. They gave her a great advantage. A previous Assemblor, a distant relative who'd owed her mother a favor, gave the priceless potion to her.

"So that's it," she said coolly and paused, trying to make him uneasy.

"They'll say you bought the data that implicates me," she said haughtily, even though she knew he could never afford that kind of information. Jury software had access to a defendant's credit history, but she had to stall him while she thought of something. *I should remove him, but surely he has foreseen that and has prepared some defense.*

Shaw quietly gazed back at her, sensing anything he said would lessen the conflict within her.

A thought came to her unbidden. If she did let him go through the gate, who was to say he could return? Inwardly she smiled.

"All right. Come back at five newHours. I will arrange it for you."

He had done it. For the first time in his life, Shaw had acted independently. He had stood up to the Assemblor, and by extension, all of society. The gentle revelations that he had leveraged and that furthered his career had become the infrastructure of any strength and ability he had as a programmer and as a *Sanjat*. From that base, and similar in kind to his other revelations, these newest ones about Smit and jazz and fears of corruption in his government and society had set him on a frightening path that led to a fearful confrontation with the most powerful woman in the Realm. Yet his feeling of the wrongness of her crime had elicited a powerful yen for justice in him that played into his desire to see the Bin and Smit.

*　　　*　　　*

The understanding came to Smit unexpectedly, its gentleness belying its depth of wisdom. This place, which he had feared all his life, was *better* than the other side. The lack of technology allowed for a more holistic and organic life flow undisturbed by the haranguing stress and turmoil of the other side. There was time, peace, and purpose here, all because of the Master's love.

Smit knew that humans designed machines to increase their leisure time and simplify life, to free people to enjoy meaningful experiences with one another. This purpose had never been realized. The more work that people delegated to machines, the harder people labored in turn. Each technological breakthrough was eclipsed by a larger development. The pace of change and the increasing sophistication of machines overwhelmed and wearied the human psyche. The pace of human life never slackened; it only increased.

Smit felt peace here. His spirit enjoyed the Bin like nourishing food.

He smiled. It hurt.

* * *

The *Sanjat* was East Indian. His great-great-great-grandfather had been an English missionary, which explained the Shaw family name. One of the missionary's two sons had not followed his father's calling. He had a gift for programming, and had been among the first East Indian computer programmers. He lived in the ancient days when companies like Burroughs, Unisys, Olivetti, and Siemens fostered and tapped the budding Indian tech pool in Bombay, and later Bangalore. His ancestor toiled with First Generation Programming Languages. By the time his forefather died, the man had advanced as far as the Fourth Generation Languages, programs that could generate code themselves. This was also the time of the genesis of object-oriented programs, with their black boxes, object modules that operated without human programmers needing to know *how* the modules operated.

Since the time of the missionary, programming held more importance than spirituality on his side of the Shaw family. Nevertheless, the *Sanjat* often wondered about God and spirituality, and his cousins who followed the missionary's way. But the *Sanjat* was always too busy to pursue this interest, and a bit frightened of it as well; God's ways might jeopardize his position. Programming was in his blood and there would be no possibility of giving it up. It was simply who he was.

As agreed, Shaw entered the Assemblor's office at five newHours. The abundance of data screens gave him a pleasurable dizziness. In this office dwelt the most advanced *accellerene* devices of his era, those that increased the speed of the electrons of matter to light speed. Thus the accelerated matter could be transported instantaneously as light.

Had he made a mistake? He loved computing and was good at it. He could have leveraged the information he had about the Assemblor into a better job, perhaps one in this very building. He might have even joined her elite team, the pinnacle of success.

"It is arranged," she said. "You go through the gate at seven. You must travel there yourself." She picked up a small grey signaling device from her desk.

"Implant this in your palm. It will allow you to return through the gate when you desire. Hold your hand up to the door. I will watch you now as you delete those files about me." She picked up a small plug. "Here, use my Interlocutor. It will know if you have any other files hidden somewhere."

*   *   *

"I can't believe this is happening," an awed Shaw said blankly. The Bin stretched before him. He saw a man sitting a short distance from the gate and realized it was Smit. He recognized him from his file holograph, but this man looked years younger. Apparently he had not wandered far from his entry point.

*   *   *

For the first time in his life, Shaw felt utter peace. He had no fear. After three days in the Bin, he had just one ambition: to reach others with the good he had experienced here.

He approached Smit: "You influenced me from afar, my friend. I had a hunger to know God, and you supplied key pieces to the puzzle of my life's spirituality. Is the Master's spirit accessible on the other side?"

Smit grinned, an expression that was no longer painful; smile muscles grew stronger with use. "Yes, His spirit is there, too. A saxophonist turned me on to it a long time ago. His name was Don."

Sanjat Shaw smiled also. "I thought that's how it happened with you." He looked out on the valley in front of them. The "fryOuts"—as they were known on the other side—seemed happy enough here. "Jazz," he said, smiling and shaking his head.

*   *   *

At seven newHours, after being in the "hell" of the Bin for three days, Shaw passed back through the gate. Until then, he wasn't sure whether the Assemblor had tricked him with an ineffective implant. But it worked seamlessly.

As he passed through, he felt as though he had found his destiny, that he had learned God's will. His

59

programming reputation would precede him, giving him a platform from which to speak.

Sanjat Shaw had a simple message to spread among the driven people on this side of the gate, one they had never heard before: Love the Master, and love others as you love yourself.

In memory of Don Lanphere, jazz saxophonist and member of Eastside Foursquare Church

Memoir

Soldier

Along with my Christian brothers and sisters from around the country, I worked long days in the sweltering New Orleans heat helping locals recover from Hurricane Katrina. Mile after mile, the city was devastated, without power, food, or water. I worked outside for only a couple of my workdays; some teams labored outdoors almost every day, including a team led by a carpenter named Steve from Redmond, Washington. One day after work, word spread that Steve's team had found an abandoned dog wandering in one of the desolate, deserted parishes. It must have been lost a long time; Katrina had ravaged the Gulf Coast region nearly a month earlier. I wasn't sure why, but they named the dog Soldier.

Soldier was a little beagle born with only three legs. He had been all by himself for so long and I couldn't comprehend how he how he had survived. Maybe that's why they called him Soldier.

Steve's team had been so moved by compassion that they brought Soldier back to the School of Urban Missions facility, which served as our headquarters during the relief effort. There they washed him and gave him food and water. Steve had even made a little dog house with an opening on one side. That first night I acquainted myself with the little guy. He lay on his side with his eyes barely open. When I touched him, he didn't move or acknowledge my presence. He looked exhausted and I didn't have much hope that he'd make it. A feeling of sadness and heaviness came over me. I had a dog of my own and I loved animals.

Before going out to work the next morning, I spent a little time with Soldier. He had changed his position during the night, so his head was facing the other way as he lay in his little house. I thought he looked marginally better, but maybe I was just relieved he hadn't died during the night, and felt a little hope. His food and water were untouched. I laid my hand tenderly on his back and then gently moved it up to his round beagle head, kind of like the head of a small, bald man, so soft and comforting to feel. I began to pray for him. I asked the Lord Jesus to breathe His life into the little dog. I tried to convey my love and concern for Soldier through my touch and through my prayer. I even told the devil that he couldn't have Soldier's life.

Something happened that I won't soon forget. As I prayed, my hand resting tenderly on Soldier's dear, vulnerable head, he looked in my eyes. Oh that I could explain that look! Of relief and mild surprise and even recognition, as if something long sought for and even given up on had finally come. The look in Soldier's eyes said: "Somebody loves me. Someone wants me. Someone wants me to live!"

We went to New Orleans to minister to hurting people who needed a reminder that there was someone who loved them. We are all looking for that love. What an honor to carry the love of God to share with others.

> *For God so loved the world that He gave His only begotten Son, that whoever believes in Him should not perish but have everlasting life...*
>
> John 3:16

Memoir

Checking Out
the French Quarter

Afeter working all day in the field, I sat down next to a lively fellow named John at dinner. Soon we were talking. He was one of three police chaplains who had come from York, Pennsylvania, to help in the relief effort after Hurricane Katrina, like I had, except I came from Seattle and wasn't a police chaplain. John was white, one of the other chaplains was black, and the third was Latino. God had assembled this team of chaplains of diverse ethnicities to come to New Orleans and minister to the bruised and brokenhearted storm victims, each chaplain's background serving as a bridge that would help in the healing that was so desperately needed.

John's "day" job was pastoring an Assembly of God church in York, which he had done for three years. Before that he had been a pastor at another church for nearly three decades. The other police chaplains from York were also pastors, and as such had experience in ministering to hurting people. It turned out that John was 63, although he could have passed for 50. This was his last night in New Orleans, and he wanted to go out on the town. He and his companions were to leave the School of Urban Missions (SUM), in Gretna, Louisiana, the next morning and head back to Pennsylvania, a 16-hour trip by van. SUM was our headquarters while we worked with the Katrina victims.

John told me stories about some of the folks he had ministered to while in New Orleans. He spoke of people who had no flood insurance, of those who had lost their homes, and of dead deer on rooftops; the deer had sought refuge from the deep floodwaters but succumbed anyway from stress and exposure. He had ministered to some of the hardest-hit people in the region.

As we talked, a couple of things became apparent: John was a jazzophile, and he wanted to visit the French Quarter before he left. He couldn't get his fellow chaplains to accompany him: One wasn't feeling well and the other was still out helping someone. He said he didn't want to go downtown alone. I silently prayed about going with him. I felt an urge to do so, despite my tiredness and a fear that a poor night's rest would make the next day in the field impossibly difficult. But while in New Orleans, I constantly felt the presence and grace of God with me, and I believe others felt it in themselves also. Every unction that motivated me to do something out of the ordinary turned out to be an incredible blessing. Somewhat nervously, I told John that I would accompany him to the French Quarter that evening, grumbling inwardly and wondering what the Lord was getting me into this time. John rejoiced at having a companion, which was at least some confirmation that I made the right choice. Thus began one of the most remarkable nights of my life.

John wore his chaplain's uniform for our excursion, which made him look like a police officer. We also rode in the chaplains' van, which looked official. John made sure to take stacks of a couple tracts that he had designed himself. One had a picture of storm damage on the front and talked of rebuilding one's house (life) on the foundation of Jesus Christ. (See Matthew 7:24-27. This is perhaps easier and less scary than it sounds: You do so by hearing and putting into practice Jesus' words, like "Love God and love your neighbor as yourself.") The other was a cool tract about how one could trade the blues for the joy of the Lord. John was especially proud of his blues tract and felt it would get good mileage around the blues clubs on Bourbon Street. I thought John did an awesome job on the tracts, howbeit the Katrina tract seemed somewhat lengthy and my experience made me doubt the efficacy of tracts in general. But I shrugged off this negativity because the Lord can use anything in a life to turn it around, and I was just along for the ride anyway. John plied me with both tracts, which I stuck in my back pockets, and he took a bunch for himself. Fully armed, we struck out for the French Quarter, he in high spirits, me a little more tentative.

After a half-hour drive from Gretna to the heart of the city of New Orleans, we were surprised at how lively the city was at night. There was an enormous camp of FEMA workers and soldiers covering several city blocks near our destination. Nearby, I saw aid workers serving meals from a long trailer. Official and regular vehicles crowded the streets. Large and small groups of people wandered about, some on missions of mercy, others receiving aid, and still others looking for a good time in the French Quarter, where many clubs and businesses remained open. It was a happening scene, and I felt a ripple of excitement that contrasted with the general oppression of the decimated area.

We passed a group of musicians playing on the front porch of a big mansion. This band, complete with a trombone player, was especially intriguing to John. He personally knew Bill Pierce, host of the Christian radio program *Night Sounds*. According to John, Pierce was one of the best trombonists in the country (I believed him). John noted the address, saying he wanted to return later. John also hoped to visit the Preservation Hall Jazz Society, which he had visited years before. Eventually we found a parking place on the curb in front of the police station near the French Quarter.

I was feeling a great deal of fear and negativity, which I later recognized as the enemy trying to keep me from a blessing. I had strange misgivings about being out of my element. I shouldn't have worried; after all, I was with a pastor of over 30 years' experience, even if he did shatter my notion of what an older pastor would be like, being much livelier than I would have expected, humorous, and full of fun. In fact, my conception of what a pastor was took quite a beating that night, in a good way. At one point, noting the scores of police on foot and all manner of police vehicles around us in the French Quarter, he leaned over to me (wearing his police-like uniform), and said quietly, "This place is just lousy with cops." John's serious appearance acted as the perfect straight man for his levity.

We paused to talk with a couple of New Orleans police officers who were tangled in conversation with an animated, intoxicated man. He openly shouted at them about the devil. They were patient with him, which I marveled at, but I was even more astounded by the theme of the conversation. In their place, I think I would have told the fellow to take a hike, or arrested him. When he finally desisted, the officers turned their attention to John and me, and were friendly and deferential. They pointed to a block party down the street, as if supernaturally guiding us, so we headed there tentatively, the live band and crowd attracting and frightening us (well, me) simultaneously. The music was not jazz or blues, which perplexed me considering our location. It sounded rather like some kind of country or rockabilly.

As we neared the large group of people at the party, a woman materialized before us and told us to follow her, as if she had been watching and waiting just for us. As she led the way into a crowd of people at the block party, John and I looked at each other and followed. Why not?

The woman deposited us in front of a well-dressed, middle-aged couple, then turning, said, "I would like to introduce you to the next mayor of New Orleans, Ms. So-and-so." (I can't remember the woman's name.) We talked to the "future mayor" and her husband, a well-heeled, greying man who conveyed the impression that he carried plenty of social and political clout. We also talked with a female uniformed police adjunct attached to the New Orleans Police homeless ministry, a good-hearted and gentle person. We drifted to other folks, talking a bit with seemingly everybody; eventually we ended up conversing with the guitarist, who was on break, though surprisingly his bandmates carried on energetically without him. Minor, inexplicable discrepancies between what seemed normal to me and the way things happened in New Orleans that night gave the evening an added surreal sensation. (Maybe the drummer would take his break next by himself and the guitarist would return to the stage to play with the others. I didn't know; I was from Seattle.)

At a table right in front of the band sat a group of unusual folks facing the crowd. They were singularly unalike in appearance, an assemblage of individuals of various ages and vestments, most prominent among them a glamorous woman attired in fine, almost comically royal raiment and coiffure. I later learned that she was 73 years old, the chief centerpiece and operator of a famous strip club in the French Quarter. She looked to be about 35 or 40, and bore a striking resemblance to Cher. Apparently the lead singer in the band, a remarkably good-looking woman, though a mediocre songstress who especially struggled with high notes, had been a former stripper in Cher's club. Based on her skimpy attire and attractive figure, her occupation hadn't seemed to change much and I surmised that a recording of her, without accompanying visuals, might not be particularly compelling or entertaining, especially to men. All this seemed quite plain to me, but other folks seemed not to notice or care. Many were well lubricated by spirits, which explained a lot.

We left the block party and interacted with whomever the Lord put in our way. John's uniform attracted people, and he was an engaging conversationalist. Eventually he would mention the Lord, but he was content to follow and enjoy the turns of conversation without pushing an agenda. Often he concluded conversations by asking if the person would like to read something he'd written (one of the tracts). People were happy to take one, often exclaiming, "You wrote this?" It was as though he had shattered their impression that all gospel tracts are written by a small group of old, white, legalistic, and bespectacled males (a fair approximation of me), who seldom venture beyond the small, dark cells where they live and toil. (They leave their cells a few times a week to attend church, buy fresh writing supplies, and replace the few, select sections of the Bibles they've worn out.)

The Preservation Hall Jazz Society was not open that night, and most of the live bands we saw in the Quarter played mediocre rock music. Musically, it was very disappointing, as it seemed the French Quarter pandered to contemporary tastes by providing music that was foreign to the New Orleans area. We did talk to a bluesman named Big Al, "424 pounds of pure blues," and he was open and kind. John gave him a blues tract, which he accepted. As we interacted with Big Al, Darrell Mansfield came to mind as a blues singer whose music was influenced by the gospel.

We found the mansion we drove past earlier, where there had been the band with the trombonist, though disappointingly, the band had gone. We approached two men talking on a veranda nearby. They confirmed that the band had indeed left for the night, and then began a conversation with us. It turned out that they were in the employ of Senator Joseph Lieberman, and one in particular seemed to have some influence. They were on a Katrina fact-finding mission, among other things. They seemed comfortable with, and even in favor of allowing the National Guard in the area. I didn't mention it, but their welcoming the National Guard conflicted with other liberal viewpoints I'd heard. I recalled hearing a nationally syndicated, liberal talk show originating in San Francisco a couple of weeks earlier in which the female host likened President Bush to Hitler for bringing in the National Guard; she was sure that he would declare martial law and begin his destruction of the democratic process. Did I really hear that? It hearkened back to the ridiculous rumors I'd heard speculating that President Bush had not only welcomed the terrorist attack on 9/11 as a means of increasing his power, but had actually secretly masterminded it.

When the unexpected and remarkable conversation with Lieberman's employees concluded (I felt like a "player," hob-knobbing with movers and shakers), we walked back the way we came, talking to people as we went: five firemen from Baltimore who were substituting for a crew in Mississippi that had to flee the flood, all of whom had apparently lost their homes, and had nowhere to go; a convenience store owner and his wife and precocious, charming three-year-old daughter; and a club bouncer who was fascinated by one of John's tracts. As we neared the van, we had the chance to pet three magnificent police horses that were tied to the station fence, their riders nowhere to be seen.

We'd had an incredible evening and were in high spirits. I had enjoyed myself and I wondered if what we had been doing could be considered working for the Lord. As we got into John's car, a police van in the crowded street waited patiently for our spot. I walked back to talk to the driver and recognized the woman who had been at the block party at the beginning of our evening, the uniformed woman who worked with the homeless. (A note about the bad press surrounding the New Orleans Police Department: can any other locality claim to have a branch of their police department devoted solely to helping the homeless, as New Orleans does?)

I made sure that she got the parking place as we left. I glanced at my watch and calculated that we would even get back in time for us to get some sleep before tomorrow's adventures. John started to drive back. After a few minutes, he stopped to consult the map, the first of a number of stops and starts on our return to Gretna. We hadn't seemed to be making much progress getting back to the freeway. As an aside, in New Orleans, locals do not call them "freeways." They are "expressways," and they have tolls in certain places. Eventually we found an expressway, but it didn't seem to be taking us back to our dormitory.

By degrees I realized that this wandering about might go on for a while, so I hazarded, "We could ask someone for directions." John turned to look at me, unsmiling. I feared I was testing our new friendship. But after several minutes the suggestion seemed to grow on him, and he grudgingly acquiesced.

We exited the expressway and headed down a main drag of New Orleans. Although the street was well lit, there were only a few other vehicles on the road. Eventually we pulled alongside a Department of Homeland Security Humvee at a light, and John motioned for the man in the passenger's seat to roll down his window. He asked the uniformed man how to get to Gretna. The light turned green, but there were no cars behind us and therefore no hurry; the city was deserted.

He paused a few moments before answering. I could almost see the wheels turning in his head as he struggled to supply an answer. I suppose it would have been rude to ask if he were from this area, though his hesitancy should have tipped us off. He told us to turn around and follow the signs to Route 10 eastbound. We did that, but as we got on the expressway, John wondered aloud if we'd been misled.

We passed exits that we had already driven by when we were lost a few minutes earlier. Then we noticed something else: There was no power on in the direction we were headed, for as far as we could see. We continued, but our confidence in these directions ebbed until we were sure they were wrong. In a few minutes, we could see nothing but black, not only in front of us, but also to each side and even behind us. We knew the power was on in Gretna, and we hadn't passed through this dark area to get to the French Quarter. We traveled on into the unknown, my stomach queasy, my fear rising.

Only our headlights pierced the darkness, and John remarked that they were either dirty or dimming because they afforded precious little light. My uneasiness grew. It was just so dark all around us. At least we were still on the expressway; how lost can you be on an expressway? Occasionally we saw other cars headed in the opposite direction. We just had to turn around and get going the other way.

I wasn't sure about John, who seemed to be as buoyant as ever, but I was scared as we proceeded further and further into the shadows of this unfamiliar, deserted land. My imagination ran wild: Were there beings out there in the dark, people, or once-domestic animals that had become wild now that there weren't any people to care for them? I really wanted to turn the car around and head the other way, back to the light, where things were familiar and safe.

We were driving toward Mississippi, parts of which, particularly near the Louisiana-Mississippi border, had been hit even harder than New Orleans. Whereas the houses in New Orleans were devastated, we had heard that residences and buildings in Mississippi were gone entirely, swept off their foundations, never to be seen again.

I ventured that in my experience, onramps were mostly on the right side of freeways. Because we needed to head the opposite way, we needed to exit the freeway, cross it under or above, and get to the other side. Then we could find an onramp. John, without comment, took the next exit.

The exit forked: The left-hand lane of the fork went up and over the expressway; the right-hand lane veered toward streets on the right (wrong) side of the freeway. John slowed the van and almost stopped as he approached the fork, uncertain which way to turn. I opined that the left fork would get us over to the other side of the expressway and then all we had to do was find an onramp. I say "opined" but I was sure God was impressing me (us) to turn left. Just before hitting the divider separating the left from the right fork, John cranked the wheel hard to the right and goosed the gas. Humbled, I consoled myself with various thoughts: John was possibly deeper in the Lord than I; John had been a pastor for a long time; and, that because with God all things are possible, maybe even though John had just turned the wrong way, God could still get us out of this. The scripture does say that He can make beauty from ashes.

As we descended to ground level (most of the expressways in New Orleans are elevated), what we saw was not pretty. In the French Quarter there had been no wind; now gusts blew trash around this forsaken, damaged, dismal part of the city in which we now found ourselves. It had been a busy, heavily populated, commercial neighborhood. Now it looked like outer darkness, the abundant signs of civilization underscoring that not a soul breathed here now. I called aloud to Jesus for help. John said Amen.

Street barricades constrained our van and John eventually turned right at a useless stop sign. As we passed under the expressway, I again felt we were making progress, heading over to the right side of the freeway where we could find an onramp.

I saw a major intersection ahead, and guessed that signs would direct us to a nearby onramp. Instead, John turned left onto a narrow side street. My sense of panic ticked up another notch.

How different I felt from an hour before, fear in the pit of my stomach sapping my confidence and joy like a deep wound. Surely this was the enemy at work.

I believed not only in a personal savior, namely Jesus, that wonderful guy, but a personal devil who was also a spirit, and who hindered our communion with others and made trouble in our lives. He also tried to keep us from the savior who loved us, and he tried to steal God's blessings. I believed these statements about the devil, not only because of my experience, but more importantly, because the Bible supports them (Matthew chapter 4). I began to see that this evening had been a great blessing in our lives (and who knows who else's life that we had encountered) and now the enemy of our souls was trying to replace our joy with fear. Fear and torment were not from God: they were either a work of the devil, or natural, and Jesus wanted people to be free of them.

Look at Psalm 40:3:

He has put a new song in my mouth—
Praise to our God;
Many will see it and fear,
And will trust in the Lord.

But how can you trust somebody whom you fear? Look at verse 4a:

Blessed is that man who makes the Lord his trust…

Again, how can you trust someone if you are afraid of them? If the Lord delights in those who trust in Him, why would He also tell us to be afraid of Him?

Answer: In verse 3 we must be talking about something other than "fear" regarding God. Here, I think "fear" means thinking of Him first, doing things pleasing to Him and believing in Him, rather than being controlled by the fear of what others may think of us; we have to get our priorities right. As the song goes, He is our audience of one.

If we lost our only orienting landmark (the expressway) or if our van broke down or ran out of gas, how would anyone find us? We were in a vast, abandoned city without power, lights, or water. Although we did not see any people or animals, someone or something was surely nearby. I conjured images of wild dogs.

We drove a while and then I saw it, a splash of green reminiscent of freeway directional signs up in the Pacific Northwest, and perhaps in John's stomping grounds in York too. The trouble with this hint of freeway-sign green was its size; it was way too small. Could it possibly help us?

"John, look, is that a directional sign?"

John drove on without responding. On closer inspection, I saw that it was a mangled green freeway directional sign, which made it appear smaller than normal. It pointed the way to the expressway. We were saved.

We both relaxed as we headed up onto the expressway, and back to our camp.

"I need to get some gas before we head back tomorrow," John said as we approached SUM, safely back in Gretna. The wind was quite strong here as well, kicking up dirt and trash around us. Like New Orleans, Gretna was deserted at this hour.

"Sounds good. There's a gas station to the left up here under the freeway," I replied, remembering it well from an unsettling experience the day before, when a huge crowd of volatile, short-tempered people swarmed inside and demanded gas from a few overwrought employees.

John pulled the van into the well-lit Shell station, but it was hard to tell if it was open. It sure looked like it, but we were the only car around. It was, however, near midnight.

John glanced over at me and asked as though he didn't actually think I would know, "Is this gas station open or not?"

We watched as a big sign, its bulk acting like the sail on a boat, its text facing the other direction, blew slowly past my door to the front of the van. It continued to slide until it was about 20 feet in front of us, at which point as though on cue it pivoted so that we could read it: "Hi. We will reopen at 8:00 AM." Trembling at God's eeriness and presence, but amused by His sense of humor, John and I returned to our dorm. It had been an evening to remember. I didn't know about John, but I was shaken up while we were lost, and I was so glad to be back.

Memoir

The Cry

One night I stumbled across a riveting criminal investigation documentary. In TV newsmagazine style, a narrator told the story of a cowardly sexual predator, cutting between investigators, police, and crime-scene locations to build tension. In some scenes, actors helped portray the events.

With growing fascination, I watched the story. The perpetrator fondled children in unoccupied toy-store aisles, and he raped a young woman. My anger grew as I watched.

The police were frustrated and under immense pressure to find the criminal before he murdered someone. They had no evidence except a string of increasingly bold and alarming crimes. Finally, they found him on a bit of video tape from a surveillance camera at a recent crime scene. It was tangible evidence, but the crimes continued unabated, and the police feared that the predator would lose control altogether.

One day the criminal abducted a young woman in a hotel, forcing her into an elevator with a gun. He planned to kidnap her and was taking her to his car. His hostage was a Christian high school student. She said later, "I knew that if I died I would go to heaven, and that gave me courage." She decided to risk breaking free, and ran for safety as he escorted her through the hotel. That decision probably saved her life. If she had not escaped at that moment, she would have been in the criminal's power completely. Her bold dash and the ensuing disturbance allowed the police to catch her abductor. By this time, I was so angry that I wanted to kill the scum myself.

I had recently watched a news clip about a man who had killed several people on Capitol Hill in Seattle. During the trial, the murderer didn't deny his horrible crimes, but his lawyer pled not guilty for him on the basis that his client had multiple personalities: seventeen of them, he said. It has always astonished me how often people who were obviously guilty avoided confessing to their crimes or showing any remorse whatsoever. The Capitol Hill killer sat stonily in court as his victims' families confronted him during sentencing, evil leering from his eyes.

On the other show, they filmed the sexual predator during his trial. What a contrast with the Capitol Hill killer: The former pled guilty, and stared miserably at the floor. He did not resist the inexorable torrent of accusations, each word making him wince. When the Christian high school student confronted him, he moaned in agony. He had been struck deeply and painfully. But his cry conveyed more than physical pain.

The sound pierced my heart, and I believe it pierced God's. God heard that cry and responded to the man. I knew *my* anger toward him turned to pity. God is so much more compassionate than I am. (I say this based on my experience and knowledge of God.) The man's crimes were horrible, but at least he realized how vile he was, how captured he'd been by his horrible sin. God responds to these awakenings and offers a solution, a way out of death's trap. (Many "good" people don't realize that compared to Jesus, they are like that man, even though they may not have sinned so horribly.) His crimes were egregious and injured vulnerable people, including children. Some of them might be in healing their whole lives. It was also right that this criminal be held accountable for his crimes and endure punishment.

But God is merciful, and if he marked sins, who could stand? Not I. In prison, God will give (even) this man a chance to start over. I hope he takes it.

The book of Proverbs is true. Verse 28:13 reads as follows:

He who covers his sins will not prosper,
But whoever confesses and forsakes them will have mercy.

Memoir

Late Bloomers

A fter my six-month contract as a contingent technical writer expired in January of 2005, I was unemployed again. People like me in the technology field were known as "contractors," and worked in several disciplines—program management, writing, editing, design, and coding, among others. Companies made a distinction between direct employees and contractors: Although direct employees' and contractors' wages were sometimes similar, there was a dramatic difference between us regarding benefits like health insurance, stock options, and other financial incentives. And of course there was the big difference that direct employees had continual employment whereas each contract lasted from weeks to months, and if I was fortunate, up to a year.

Being periodically unemployed was typical for contractors, and if I had lived in a social vacuum, I wouldn't have had a problem with it. After six years of contracting, most of my discomfort from periods of no work stemmed from family and friends, who could not help but see unemployment as a stigma (which they handily attached to me), probably because of their unfamiliarity with the business practices of the Information Age. As the old song title says, it was "Kind of a Drag."

Back when I had been contracting and it seemed like I'd be getting paychecks forever, I had bought my one and only new car for my wife and me, a 2004 Toyota Camry. Our euphoria quickly evaporated. The car's mechanical problems irritated me for months, particularly because Toyotas were supposed to be immune to these troubles. Getting repairs while working had not been easy.

Between the job and my commute, I was away from home 12 hours per day and I had little time or energy to haggle with the auto dealership. Eventually I managed to contact them, and they told me that making an appointment on Saturday was out of the question for vague, unchallengeable reasons. I would have to bring the car in on a weekday, which meant that I had to take time off work. Great.

This car had several issues: There was an annoying rattle in the ceiling by my left ear that I couldn't locate or fix. Clear, unsightly plastic stuck out from under the doorplates on both sides of the front seats. A sound like a banshee came from what I guessed was the left-front wheel well when I drove 40 miles-per-hour or faster, scaring and distracting me. There was a trail of dried-looking stuff on the valve cover gasket that looked like gasket seal. These kinds of things aren't so bad in a used car. But in a new car, at $376.09 a month for the next five years, these flaws took on a dark, mocking life of their own. They ate at me, though I'll admit that work-related stress probably magnified these defects.

Naturally, of the five grievances that I brought to the dealership's attention, they fixed only one completely. So I had this new car that annoyed me, and now I was unemployed and couldn't afford the payments. I decided to drive the car to the dealership, talk to them, and evaluate my options.

I ended up selling the car back to them, which almost covered my loan from Toyota. Between the down payment and my monthly payments, I had deposited eight grand into a dark hole, never to be seen again, and after taking the car back all we had to show for it was the end of those burdensome monthly payments, which was something at least. Unfortunately, we now had no car. I didn't urgently need one, and my wife took the bus to work. But getting groceries and going to church required us to walk or get a ride, and if I got an interview I had to take the bus. We had a good transit system here, but it took substantially longer to get everywhere.

About 25 years ago, I met an African-American man named Cordell at church, and we became fast friends. Whenever I was around him or his mother, I felt different and a little more in touch with the perspective of a black person. For five years I had lived in the inner city and had been about the only Caucasian at the Pentecostal church I attended. I had a bit more experience living with blacks than most whites had, but I was also aware that I really had no clue what it was like to be black. My friend Ben, who married an African-American woman, knew infinitely more about this than I did. His skin would never be black, which was reason enough for some blacks to hate and exclude him; his marrying a black woman and having a mixed family were similarly taboo for some whites. I suppose the gap between whites and blacks has been bridged some, but not much.

Cordell called me one day recently and asked if I wanted to go to a free dinner with him and his mother at a church on Capitol Hill. I expressed my interest, and he came over and picked me up. There were a number of homeless people and others who didn't receive much income at the church, and the servers were from the Catholic Workers group. The day went pretty well, but it was humbling. Life doles out big changes. A few months earlier, I had been eating scrumptious feasts with "players" in the high-tech community in company-subsidized restaurants. Now I was eating donated food, much of it past its pull date, with the unemployed (like me) and homeless. Like most of the folks around me, I didn't own a car.

Cordell had taken an indefinite leave of absence from his job as a teacher's aide to take care of his mother Geneva, who had Alzheimer's. He took her everywhere he went, including to school when he was getting his master's. He was even on TV recently, on a Christian station late at night, being interviewed about how he took care of her rather than put her in a home. He didn't care for her for what he could get out of it, telling the reporter, "She took care of me when I couldn't take care of myself; I'm just returning the favor."

Time had mellowed and added sweetness to the old woman. Geneva had no rough edges, and was patient and gracious. She completed those in her company, if one were open and patient, though to some she was just a burdensome old woman.

When we went back to the house he and his mother shared, he asked me if I could help him move some stuff out of his '87 Honda Accord. He pulled the car out back and we transferred the items to one of two other cars parked in the back, both of which were essentially immobile. For whatever reason, he hung on to an aged, broken-down Mazda station wagon and a big, ancient, ramshackle Buick that his mother used to drive.

Cordell always went to the same mechanic and the Mazda, back when he used to use it, seemed like it was perpetually in the shop with problems. He would have one problem fixed and pay the mechanic in installments, and then something else would happen to the car and he'd have to have *that* fixed so he could get to work. The problems and payments went on for years. For all I knew, he was still making payments to that mechanic for a car that was no longer drivable. He probably put one of the mechanic's kids through college. I could relate to why he didn't want to get rid of these vehicles: A car is one of the few things in this world that you can invest in continually and still come away with nothing. He probably couldn't bear to see the thousands of dollars he'd spent on repairs simply towed off his driveway.

When we were done moving the stuff, he brought a vacuum and extension cord out, "plugged it up," in Cordell's parlance, and asked if I could vacuum the trunk. I obliged, and then he asked if I could vacuum the rear seats and floor in the back. I did, and then he asked me to get the front also. I was annoyed and wanted to go home and watch TV with my wife, but I did it anyway, showing just a hint of attitude. All this time he was hustling around, doing different tasks on the cars and in other places. Finally, we were done. We went inside and talked to his mother for a while, and then it was time for me to go. I had been patient, waiting for him to take me home, a captive worker until then.

We got as far as the front porch before he turned to me, smiling: "Here you go," he said, holding out the Honda key. I stared at him blankly. "The only thing I ask is that you get the car back to me by the weekend so I can do my shift at Domino's. I don't use the Cadillac for that," he said chuckling, referring to his other running car. He had bought it for a friend with the understanding that the friend's mother would pay him for the car; she didn't, so he kept it. He couldn't really afford it, but at least it turned out to be convenient for driving his mother around. She could get in and out of the Cadillac easier, though she still needed Cordell's assistance.

By degrees I realized that he was offering to let me use his car. A kind of warm shock replaced my irritation at helping him clean it. All the work I'd done was for me. That was Cordell. (Earlier that night, while we were cleaning out the trunk, he found three new stuffed teddy bears in a bag. "Does your wife want these?" he asked after discovering the bears. I said maybe just one. Later when I got in the car to drive it home, I saw that he had strapped one of the bears into the passenger seat with the seat belt. That too was Cordell.)

"I thought the Lord would have told you while you were working on it," he said, smiling. Cordell lived to spring little surprises like this.

"Well, He didn't," I admitted, thankful for the lack of a prophetic tip. I had enough trouble without trying to carry a prophet's mantle around the narrow confines of my rut. The Lord did speak to me on occasion, but I rarely knew how to respond, exactly.

When I was with Cordell, or when my wife and I visited him and his mother, he was ever the servant, seldom sitting down as he moved about, tending to our various needs, and never forgetting his mother: *Would you like some juice? Let me show you this picture. Are you hungry? Mother, will you take your medication now?* He wasn't busy; he just calmly tended to various things, most of them for other people. He had no hint of attitude about serving others. Some people made you aware of the pains they were taking for you—Cordell did not. I think he got this from the Lord Jesus. One of the fruits of God's spirit was humility: If we allowed the Lord's spirit to abide in us, nice things grew inside us of their own accord. There was an old gospel hymn I used to hear in the black church named "Let God Abide." Would you? Could I?

As I drove the Honda home, I noticed a smell of fumes, not quite raw gas, more like a diesel smell, though Honda had never made a diesel to my knowledge. I thought then that while I had the car, I should have a mechanic look at the problem. I prayed about it and seemed to get the go-ahead, but as usual, it was kind of hard to tell. The next day I called up a well-known Honda repair shop—not a dealership, they charged too much—to make an appointment. They couldn't see the car until after Labor Day, so I would need to return it to Cordell for his Domino's shift on Saturday, and then we'd have to take the car down several days after. I did wash the Honda before taking it back, something Cordell noticed: "Thanks for giving my car a bath." A day or so later he asked, "Did I ever thank you for washing my car while you had it?"

When my wife and I got back to our house on Labor Day evening, Cordell had left a message on our answering machine about taking the car down to the mechanic's, and thank God it wasn't his usual mechanic, but the one I suggested. I returned Cordell's call after we got home and reached him on his cell phone. I heard a cacophony of noise in the background, the loudest a voice speaking indistinctly. Cordell was with a friend in a car, multitasking—talking to me (sort of), driving, talking to his friend, listening to a radio show, parking the car, and who knows what else. I explained where the mechanic's was and gave him the time of our appointment. He intended to drive the Honda there, leave it, and then I'd take him home. They'd call with an estimate after they diagnosed the problem.

The next morning, after not nearly enough sleep, I drove my wife to work on my way to the mechanic's so she wouldn't have to take the bus. I planned to run these errands and then get some rest. Traffic southbound on I-5 was a bearcat, as usual, and I remembered why I chose to commute before seven AM back when I'd had a job. After suffering through traffic, stressed because I thought I'd be late, I dropped her off and found the mechanic's shop on Denny Way. I waited nearly 20 minutes for Cordell, and started to get irritated. I'd forgotten to bring his cell number so I couldn't call him, and the receptionist wasn't crazy about letting me use his computer to access my Hotmail account, where I could retrieve the number. Just when I had resigned myself to losing the long-awaited appointment, he drove up; he had gone to another branch of the same mechanic's franchise.

On our way back to Cordell's house, he told me about his nephew, the son of his sister, Ellen. Ellen and her husband were teachers. She had dropped her son off at Cordell's house several days earlier, having prepaid him to paint the steps on one of the outdoor staircases. He disappeared on Capitol Hill that afternoon, and did not show up for another three days. He was addicted to crack cocaine, so his behavior, while disappointing and troublesome, was not altogether surprising. Cordell marveled that his sister would actually pay him for the job in advance, and criticized her for it, hoping she'd learned a lesson.

When we got to the house, Cordell invited me in. I was ready to go home and get some sleep, but I could tell he wanted me to come in. His mother liked me and it helped him and her to have some company during what must have been long and difficult days for them. As we walked into the living room, I saw the nephew stretched out on the couch in front of the TV, Cordell's mother sitting to our right, closer to the set in her own chair. Now I realized why Cordell had been talking about him in the car. I hadn't realized that he was actually at their house. Like everyone in Cordell's family, the nephew was slim and tall, with a narrow face and fine features. He wore dark pants and an unzipped jacket. He awoke and drifted off intermittently.

The next time he surfaced, Cordell introduced us. The nephew, whose name was Marques, said hi and almost immediately fell asleep again. He was on his back, with his thin legs propped up on the far armrest, light, almost-white socks clashing with what little fashion integrity his other garments afforded. The socks transfixed me, their garish appearance emblematic of the chaos in Marques's life. I wondered how old he was. I tried to estimate by guessing Ellen's age. He could have been 35.

In my experience, many of my black acquaintances were careful about what they wore; Marques, by contrast, did not appear concerned about his wardrobe, at least in his present circumstances. He looked uncomfortable, waking periodically, never lucidly. I saw Cordell's mother look at him, and then turn away, her eyes hard, an ill-concealed expression of disgust etched on her face. I could actually *see* the burden he had on Geneva, how Marques was straining unbreakable family ties to the limit. Here was a man with wants and needs and a life that God had granted him, worthy of respect and compassion like any other man. And yet there was a hook in him, driving all his actions and thoughts, perhaps even tainting his personality and eclipsing his humanness in our minds at times, and maybe even in his. After a while, I went for the door. I wasn't disgusted and tried not to judge the man. But I felt the horrible burden of him through my friends. Drug addiction had struck me deeply through friends and family, but it had not left me bitter. But neither had it wounded me recently. Maybe I would be bitter if it had.

Cordell brought his mother outside, and they walked me to the car. My wife and I had just bought a '95 Buick LeSabre from one of her relatives a few days earlier, right after Cordell had loaned us his Honda. Cordell thought his mother would like to see it, and he wanted to get her away from Marques for a minute. Cordell also wondered if his mother could ride in it when I took him down to pick up the Honda. Their family had an attachment to Buicks. She had driven one to the Northwest from North Carolina in the '50s (which gave me some vague allusion to a modern-day, African-American covered wagon in my unusual thinking), and then another one during the many years that she worked at Sears. That particular Buick was out back, the one Cordell couldn't seem to part with. Funny how something that was once top-of-the-line could look so funky now.

"He's still coming down from those drugs," Cordell said, not needing to refer to Marques specifically, the heaviness of his nephew on us like his very presence since we left the house.

I looked at him. "I didn't know he was *here*. When did he come here?"

"This morning," Cordell said. "Ellen dropped him off on her way to work. She wants him to finish the porch, seeing how he's already been paid for it." I felt the immediacy of this new burden on Cordell and his mother now that he was at their house, but also the continuous and perhaps eternal weight on his sister. There wasn't much to say because they didn't complain.

I suggested we pray, and they agreed. "Let's pray in the car," he said.

Cordell situated his mother in front and got in back. "Oh, this car is so nice," Geneva said, looking around at the feature-rich interior of the LeSabre. "Really nice, I like it." The car did have every imaginable option, including leather seats. I was beginning to warm up to it, and it was noticeably more opulent than the Toyota in an Americana, 1995-kind of way.

"Where does he live?" I asked, getting back to Marques.

Cordell shrugged. "I don't know. My sister's husband won't allow him over there anymore. Too much stuff was coming up missing."

I started praying: "Lord, thank you for this nice day and for all your blessings. We praise and thank you. You can do anything, and nothing's too hard for You. We lift up Cordell's nephew to You. This drug addiction seems so heavy to us, but it's nothing to You. You can deliver him from it. We ask You to do that." I forget exactly what else I said, but Cordell prayed a bit along these lines as well. We finished up and Cordell helped his mother back inside.

I drove home, slept for a couple hours, woke up, and poured myself a cup of coffee. I noticed that the answering machine was blinking. The mechanic had left a message saying that their estimate was complete and to call him back, which I did. The work to eliminate the fumes consisted of three tasks totaling $1,072. Seriously. That was just to replace three fuel injectors and fix two oil leaks. One of the oil leaks was the valve cover gasket, and the other was the O-ring on the distributor, neither of which seemed particularly difficult to fix. Of course, I had no heart to attempt that work myself. The injector work alone was $800.

I called Cordell and explained that I probably wouldn't be able to afford to have the car fixed, and waited for his reaction. He agreed that it was too pricey. He seemed to take it pretty well. "The car may not even be worth much more than that," he said mercifully. I went back to Cordell's and then I drove him and his mother down to pick up the Honda again, taking them in our Buick to please Geneva. I paid the diagnostic fee, $88 counting tax, about a fourth of my weekly unemployment check, with no repair work done on the car. Easy come, easy go.

I was disappointed that my attempt to help Cordell with his car had gone nowhere. I felt like I had gone back on my word because it cost too much. But before I drove Cordell and his mother to the mechanic's, right after they had returned from dropping off Marques in the University District, I shared a meal with them. To this day, I have chosen to remember that part of the day. It was emblematic of the time I spent with them because it was more significant than the negative and adverse circumstances and burdens that often came into our lives.

Cordell had asked me on the phone before I came over if I was hungry. I'd said not really, but by the time I had driven over there I was ready to eat something. Cordell, thoughtful as ever, had prepared lunch.

As I parked, I noticed that Marques had indeed painted the front steps of the house before he left, so that was encouraging. Hopefully the effort partially lifted the burden he placed on Cordell and Geneva, though I doubt it seldom left Ellen.

A man and his mother: *What is this relationship? What does a man owe his mother? Was Marques's relationship with Ellen driven by these obligations? Were we talking about a duty or a feeling? Were the acts of duty propelled by some emotion?* I thought of my mother. It was not a simple, surface notion. The Bible just said to honor mother and father. That made it simpler. I owed my parents honor. I wondered how to do that. Cordell's honor for his mother had substance.

Cordell's house was old, and he guessed that it had been built in the 1890s. It was technically Geneva's house, and he paid her a bit of rent in exchange for living downstairs. Once his mother got sick, he began spending more time upstairs, though I think he still slept downstairs.

The house was on a good-sized lot right in the heart of the Central District. Some of the houses in his neighborhood had been bought by young, urban professionals, and had been remodeled or rebuilt altogether. Fortunately, most of them retained their character and roots. A fence surrounded Cordell's house, and plenty of green grew on the fence and in the yard, suggesting a cloistered garden. Big, thorny rose bushes, with their sweet fragrance, bloomed here and there among the other plants and shrubs, looking more like little rose trees. One had several white blooms on it. I smelled one, getting a pleasing whiff of that delicate rose smell.

Geneva sat outside not far from their front gate. I sat down beside her while Cordell prepared our food in the upstairs kitchen.

"Gustus bought this house," she said, referring to her late husband Augustus, who passed 30 years earlier. Apparently Cordell was a junior because she always called him Gustus too. I can't ever remember her calling him "Cordell" in the 25 years I'd known her. "He sold his night club and his store and bought me this house," she continued.

"That's good. That's better than installments," I said. As I thought about Geneva's husband, I remembered that a couple of days before, Cordell had shown me a picture of his dad and several other men in front of the night club, the one he had sold to buy this house. The first thing that surprised me was that of the five men, two were Asian, perhaps Filipino. Of the three black men, it wasn't hard to pick out Cordell's slender father. One of the others was nondescript, but the third looked familiar, and it bothered me that I couldn't place the face.

"They had a special on PBS about that guy," Cordell had said, pointing to the familiar face. "He was a boxer," he said, clenching the ID.

"I saw that special," I said, recalling it. It was a film by Ken Burns, who also directed a series of jazz documentaries and other films for PBS. "I think the special was called *Unforgivable Blackness*. I think his name was Johnson." I wasn't sure of the name until I looked it up later, though. I was impressed: The man was famous, a hugely successful prizefighter whom whites could not defeat for decades, a predecessor of Muhammad Ali. While I applauded the gains Jack Johnson made for his race, I was concerned for his salvation, as I am for anyone of any race. Johnson's outward behavior, especially toward women, didn't seem to suggest he knew the Lord, at least during the early part of his life. Of course, repentance is open to all, and I didn't know whether he developed a relationship with the Lord in his later years.

Geneva, in the garden now, looked around. She was happy and content. I said, "I think I'll go up and see how Cordell is doing." I never called him Gustus; I would feel funny calling him that.

I walked up the other staircase, the one that hadn't been painted. It was only about 20 feet behind the front one, and stretched the same direction, toward the back of the house, but it was longer and steeper because the house was like a split-level. (I say "like" because it was built half a century before the term was coined.) Their property sloped down toward the back of the lot.

Marveling at its steepness, I took my time as I climbed the steps for the first time. At the top was a low entryway that I had to duck a bit to squeeze under. I entered in the kitchen on the second floor at the back of the house. It was a sunny September day, warm for that time of year, but not like the oppressively humid August heat. There was something less substantial about it, a harbinger of fall and winter's dreadful weather.

The sunshine tumbled into a small, pleasant alcove off the kitchen. I stepped into the nook and looked out the windows at the city of Seattle standing in the distance in the sunshine, and at the cozy alcove, full of sun that a yuppie might have killed for. They'd probably buy the property and renovate the house, if not tear it down altogether, for the vision of that alcove in the sun.

"Wow, this is really nice," I remarked. I didn't hear a reply. Maybe I was also a yuppie in spirit.

I went back to the kitchen and watched as Cordell cooked hotdogs and readied our salads. He primarily bought prepared foods from all sorts of different places, favoring food near its pull date. It was good food, though, bought at bargain prices or received free, helping him save money for bills and other expenses.

I looked around the old kitchen. The floor was not level, slanting to the north. Cordell's room downstairs was a hazard, full of boxes of stuff and unboxed clutter that necessitated pathways to walk through. There was less junk upstairs, but the rooms clearly hadn't received much attention recently. Nobody had the time or the money, or for that matter, the inclination to clean it up. Until Cordell took his leave of absence, he had been working one full-time and two part-time jobs, in addition to getting a master of education degree on nights and weekends. My mom was a neat freak, but these days I just didn't care. It really didn't bother me anymore.

I noticed that in the dining room off the kitchen, the big table was set nicely with placemats, plates, and silverware, as if a big group was expected that afternoon, though I knew that Cordell and his mother hadn't entertained like that for many years. The sturdy wooden chairs had blue cloth covers on the back, and one of them said "Pastor." I made a comment about it and Cordell said that it was his sister's handiwork. I guessed that Ellen had set the table, maybe as part of an anti-Alzheimer's strategy to perk up the place. I didn't think she went to church though, as Cordell did, but I could have been wrong. They had all grown up

Catholic, until Cordell was saved as a young man. Now he went to a Pentecostal church with his mother.

"What do you want to drink?" he asked me, opening the refrigerator, revealing an assortment of food. I opted for lemonade. It came in a pop can, and I didn't have high expectations for it, but found that it was pretty decent, not too sweet, with no carbonation and no weird aftertaste. "I guess I'll go down and see how your mom is doing," I said.

"She may be out pulling dandelions in the front of the house," he said, "in case you don't see her."

I walked down the steep narrow stairs and found that her seat was indeed empty. I peeked around the vinery on the front fence and saw her coming, which eased my concern. She stepped through the front gate and sat down again. "I was just pulling some dandelions," she said, confirming Cordell's guess. I looked around. It was pleasant in the garden, delightfully shaded from the sun by trees, fragrant flowers, and soothing plants. Again I got the impression that Geneva was happy, and her face looked soft. She smiled.

I looked up and saw a green trellis arching over me. A climbing plant clung to it. I hadn't even noticed it until then, and remarked on it. Geneva said her daughter had put up the trellis. Green tendrils wove in and out of the trellis, and as I looked over my head again, I saw a lovely, orange flower, something like an orchid, but smaller and the petals more delicate. Looking to the left, I saw another, and a number of buds around the flower. I admired it, and saw there would soon be more. It was September. The plant that leaned on the trellis was a late bloomer. The appearance of the vines and flowers reminded me of my wife's clematis, which she started as a small plant years ago, and it had grown each year and was now draped over our fence for 30 yards, its thick garment of leafy vines and pale blue flowers cheering up our springs. It was a wonderful plant, but those flowers did not last much past the beginnings of summer. There was a bit of pressure to enjoy them while they lasted, and in the back of my mind each spring as I looked at the clematis, I was a bit sad about their brief lifespan, even as I saw them blooming in front of me.

But this vine in Cordell's yard was just coming into its own, late in the season. Then, because of God's grace, I thought of Cordell and his mom and me, and even his nephew Marques, as late bloomers. We just had to wait a bit till our season was fully come.

Memoir

Ducklings

It was 5:45 PM when I saw them through the windshield of my car, grouped together two feet off the busy arterial, huge, heavy cars and trucks moving obliviously by: seven baby ducks huddled in a tight, inward-facing circle, trying to move forward against one another, shaking and terrified, tightening their small circle. One of them, no longer recognizable, lay in the street three feet away, a red, wet pancake of feathers and guts. It was this they feared and smelled: death in the air, near, unknown and yet instinctually recognizable, oppressing them and from which they had to escape. But they didn't know how to get away or where to turn for help. No adult ducks were in sight; apparently they were orphans. Maybe the dead one in the street had been their mother, sacrificing her life as she tried to protect them.

My heart ached watching the little ducks' panic. The sight troubled and disoriented me, dislodging my focus of getting home after work, and evaporating my weariness and self-pity. As usual I'd had a hard week documenting software. And I had just driven over to Aurora Avenue North from the Eastside in Friday afternoon traffic, a full hour trip after a tedious day. I wanted to finish my errand on Aurora, go home, eat dinner, and escape into a movie for an hour and a half with my wife, our usual Friday night fare. Now this.

I didn't stop, which would have been difficult in the heavy traffic. I drove to a nearby PetSmart, which had a small veterinary clinic attached. I explained the ducklings' plight to the sympathetic young woman at the vet's. She couldn't help me, but gave me a list of numbers to call. After exhausting the list, I wasn't any nearer to helping them. I left regretfully, full of bitterness and frustration. My frail efforts had done nothing.

I could have found a box, drove back and tried to gather the ducklings into it, and then driven over to the Humane Society on the Eastside, leaving the traumatized little creatures at a place where they knew how to care for them. I couldn't muster the strength for the effort because of my fatigue and fear of the unknowns, however. How would I drive with seven ducks in the car through rush hour traffic for an hour or more? Could I even get them in the car? The ducklings were right next to a very busy street, after all. It was too overwhelming to deal with.

I continued on to my errand. By chance there was a small vet next door to the shop. I walked in and explained about the ducklings again. The woman was sympathetic and called Animal Control for me. This was better, but did little to assuage my conscience. It was after six now, after business hours, which probably explained why I'd had so little success with the numbers I tried after my first trip to a vet.

I finished my errand and returned home. After telling my wife about what I had seen and felt, I quickly forgot about the ducklings. I had enough other things to worry about.

I had gotten in the habit of leaving early in the morning to beat the traffic on my way to work. Starting early saved me a good half hour of enervating frustration. About two weeks after the incident with the ducklings, I got in the car and drove to work early, as usual.

No one was around on the fourth floor—not the guy I shared an office with, no one in the offices to either side of me or across the hall. I turned my computer on and began working.

For the first time in a while, I began to think about the ducklings. I started to weep. They were so pitiful. I thought of their distress and need for help. They had been helpless, young, in need of a savior, and I had failed them. My vain attempts soothed my conscience not a whit. From their perspective, my efforts—calling agencies and what not—made no difference, as if I had done nothing at all, abdicating the problem. As this poignant vision of the ducklings riveted my attention from my work, wave after wave of compassion for the little guys swept over me, bringing uncontrolled, wracking sobs. At times, I was self-conscious about my crying and tried to muffle it; at others I was more cavalier. What did I care if people heard me? At times I even felt that it was important that my co-workers felt what I felt.

*　　　*　　　*

Before working in software, I was a Metro bus driver. I worked nights, and my wife Donna and I had only one car. One night, Donna came to pick me up after work. In the passenger's seat, in a box, was a little black puppy. He looked so tentative and vulnerable. Donna knew I dreamt of getting a boxer after we moved from our apartment to a house with a yard. After work she had driven up north and bought this little dog for me. It turned out that he was only half boxer, but that was just fine. We loved our unique mongrel puppy all the more.

He was unsure of his new surroundings, riding in the car, and surveying his new digs when we got home. We got ready for bed, and put him in the kitchen with a makeshift fence blocking his access to the living room and carpet.

I went to bed, but the puppy's moans kept me up, removing every bit of peace, much less sleep. It was a being's primal cry for his mother, for belonging and love and comfort. On the radio they said you had to let children cry a few nights until they build up enough emotional calluses to sleep through the night. As I heard the little puppy's wails, I started crying. I had never heard anything so forlorn that grabbed my affections like that.

I put a mat down in the kitchen and slept there with the little waif that first night. He eventually got some sleep lying up close against my chest. My being there helped him a little. That little doggie became our beloved Buster.

Buster is old now, and he has cancer. The once-jet-black hair on his face has turned white, like an aged man's beard. His hindquarters are failing him and I carry a sad, heavy burden as I watch him struggle day after day. There's nothing I can do about it. He has his adequate days and his bad days. A while ago, his back legs collapsed as he walked up the two low steps of our back porch. Sometimes he yelps when this happens, but this time he just looked at me as he fell back onto the grass. I began to cry. I pray every day for the strength and to know the right time to put him down.

About ten years ago, a saleswoman came to our home and because Buster was half boxer, she made a connection with a boxer she had owned once. She described the experience and the look on her beloved boxer's face when he was hit by a car and died looking at her, questioning and disbelief and fear in his eyes.

I watched a special on the war in Iraq. Someone casually shot a dog, for no apparent reason, and the camera recorded it up close. The dog had just been sniffing around, carefree, bothering no one. At first the dog was surprised and energetic as blood spurted from his chest. He tried to fight it by moving around. As his strength ebbed, he became resigned and lay down. That is my only memory from the TV program that was full of war and death. The dog was innocent and knew nothing about politics.

One Sunday we went up to the family picnic at the farm. My wife's Uncle Carl is a full Swede, a giant former logger with a tender heart. He had a dog named Big. Big died two weeks ago. The dog went down to a nearby creek and dug himself a little bed behind a tree. He lay down in it and died with his legs stretched out. He knew his time had come. I felt sad and wondrous listening to that story, and felt something of God in it, even if it was a bit depressing and grotesque. Carl described the dog's death in his soft, matter-of-fact tone, but I knew he was grieving and questioning it also. Carl was in Africa, in Libya, with the Air Force in 1952 when he picked up a virus that gave him a stroke; he was only 22.

Carl was in that hospital for six months, and the bug has plagued him from time to time all these years. Spending all that time in the hospital probably made his heart so tender. He's big. He was working as a logger when a choker cable snapped and hit him in the leg, breaking his thighbone. My dad said he was lucky to be alive. Carl tried to work after that, but he broke the thick steel rod they had put in his leg to hold the bone together. I've seen the rod. Apparently it had a lot of force put on it as Carl worked, and that's what made it break. I don't think he did much logging after the second operation to replace the broken steel rod.

When I was 11 and lived in Ohio, I had a dog I loved. He was a wild fella, but we were buddies. He'd come back from an adventure at the creek about a quarter mile from our house in the country, full of burrs and fun and devilment, all wet from swimming in the water. We had to clean him up. He loved adventure, smiling all the while as we scolded and cleaned him. He knew we loved him. It would snow hard there, and sometimes we'd get out of school, and our dog would jump around in the two-feet-deep snow like a lunatic, hopping from place to place because the snow was too deep to run through. One day my mom innocently let him out after I left for school. He walked up to the bus stop right after I boarded the bus, and apparently caught my scent. He ran after me and got caught under the bus's big rear double wheels. I remember some kids talking animatedly in the back of the bus, but I didn't know what they were talking about. We arrived at the first school the bus stopped at every day. The principal, Mr. Stovall, took me off the bus as it continued on to my school. He informed me that my dog had died trying to follow the bus.

Mr. Stovall and I had clashed on occasion, but I forgot all about our previous altercations as I sat in his olive-green, '50s-era car with its round hood and trunk as he drove me to my school. I was an open wound, too stunned to put much effort into crying, though tears streamed down my cheeks. At last, with heroic effort, I said weakly, "I don't think I can face the kids…" I managed to state this dry fact; I wasn't making an argument. I remember him glancing at me as he drove, and then he decided to take me home instead of to school. Maybe that was the most compassionate thing Mr. Stovall ever did. It helped me, though I didn't fully appreciate it at the time. Maybe it was God who moved him to take me home. I think I recall that his eyes were moist too, hearing me cry. I simply could not have functioned at school.

When I got home I remember I was sitting on the toilet with the door closed, crying. I don't remember if my pants were up or down. My mom came to the door and called to me, and then opened the door and came and hugged me right there on the commode as I sobbed.

*   *   *

I was an adult now and my dad was in his 80s. I saw him cry only twice in my entire life, and the second time he merely wiped his wet eyes. That first time was as he buried our little doggie in the back yard, that day that was the worst of my young life. I saw him cry from the house. I wasn't back there, though. I couldn't bear to see that. He put him in a shoebox and buried him with a shovel. I couldn't bear to see my dog dead, and my dad didn't give me the opportunity.

The ducklings. I went to the bathroom down the hall at work, weeping as I went. I wanted no one to see, and I wanted everyone to see. I didn't run into anybody. I realized that this was a God event, that God was letting me know that my feeling of compassion for those little ducks was the same way he felt for people, that all of humankind faces inward in a small circle, terrified and traumatized, desperate for help, for love and belonging and comfort, and that the strange though eerily familiar scent of death is in the air. God is our Dad, and He cares, and lots of people don't even know He is there, or can believe He cares about what has happened to them in their lives. He is there. He is here. He is not a tough judge in heaven waiting to slap us down, but that infinitely more than the way I felt that day about the ducklings, He yearns after us and wants to help us.

I've mentioned some random, poignant experiences I've had. You no doubt have your own.

Back there in the garden something really bad happened. (Crosby, Stills, and Nash sang about it.) It is really understated these days, but I don't think we can imagine what really went down, how bad it was. SOMETHING REALLY BAD HAPPENED.

Almighty God, having all power, somehow still had to suffer unimaginably to set things right. I didn't help those ducklings, but God did whatever it took to help us. He didn't say, "Oh I really tried to help. I did my best. It wasn't quite enough. Sorry about that." Jesus saves us because everything on Earth is so messed up, and we truly need Help, capitalized because "His help" is the only kind that is effective for the kind we need. If you accept and embrace Him, you'll still have pain, but you'll have the truest and most faithful of friends, in this life and the next.

The Exchange

Nate had issues, and at times it was apparent that he wasn't a very nice person. His disposition hung like an amorphous fog, a given in the life that he lived and labored under. He countered this given with the defense that at times, at least he was truthful (not the same as being honest).

In the mornings he felt terrible. But if he could escape his bed by hook or crook, get some caffeine, and get rolling on some project or platonic, self-aggrandizing goal, he had a decent chance of moving past the oppressive thoughts that camped like unwelcome and unwashed squatters among the rocks and crooks and crannies in his mind's landscape. That region was dangerous to visit alone. But he rarely had anyone who would join him there, and it was where he found himself pretty much continually.

And there was his truck, at once dead weight and irreplaceable. His truck was old and small, but something of a collector's item. Yes, in his mind it was a collector's item. But he also hated it, other times, realizing it was an old truck, an oil-burner. Nobody would call it a babe magnet, either. He liked girls, enough at times to put great thought and effort into attracting one, but he hadn't been successful.

He was a lousy driver. He had the mechanics down, but battled through bouts of road rage and constantly yelled at other drivers—especially those with nice cars—making him a competitive, rude motorist, and at times a violent and dangerous tornado on the roadway.

Nate went through his life with very little hope and even his dreams, if you could call his momentary wishes for something better dreams, were unimaginative and lacked ambition. Really his dreams consisted only of wanting to get by, or to have this or that problem gone.

Then there was a change. A person came into his life. We'll call him The Stranger. No, The Stranger was not the long-awaited dream girl. It wasn't that.

But there was no denying change had come. The advent of The Stranger was real and it appeared to be positive. Quite often a dramatic change came into Nate's life, but usually for the worse. The more he became familiar with this change, the more positive it became.

An aspect of his life was now very different, and unlike the crushing-disappointment or severe-trouble kind of change that had at times embroiled his life, this change, though radical, had a positive gentleness and subtlety.

So he watched it, half-expecting, half-dreading that it would reveal itself as another trouble, its only difference being that it had been disguised longer.

The Stranger started talking to him one day in a mini-mart. Nate wanted coffee, and he didn't have enough money. Behind him in line at the cash register, The Stranger paid his tab. They began talking.

For a week or so they got to know one another.

The Stranger saw Nate's truck and made him an offer. He asked Nate if he wanted something better to drive. Nate, defensively, asked him what he meant. The Stranger pointed to a new Cadillac parked on the street in front of Nate's small apartment. It was one of the new smaller ones that, though luxurious, got great mileage. Style *and* economy. Nate wondered what the catch was; no catch, said The Stranger.

The night before, Nate had contemplated suicide. Maybe it was these thoughts that motivated him to actually consider the trade, to take the risk that this too might crumble. Compared to suicide though, with this exchange there wasn't much to lose.

But then he had a shock: He wouldn't just gain a nice car. He would have to give up his truck, the definition of who he was, as humble and smelly as that might be. It wasn't much, but it was all he had. Give that up? Not so easy.

Thinking only of the suicide, though, and how close he had been to that terrifying act that drew him inexorably in a way he seemed powerless to resist, he realized that unless he came to terms with that, somehow held it at bay, it would engulf him and he would lose everything. He really needed something or someone to hold it off for him. So he leaped at The Stranger's offer. He traded pink slips with The Stranger that afternoon.

Man what a nice car! He didn't even think about other drivers in that Cadillac, like he had before, when he felt the bitterness and competition, feeling that others were trying to cut him off and take his rights. Maybe Nate absorbed something of The Stranger as he drove his new car. The Stranger was such a nice person.

Then one day, as he waited in a long line near the freeway, a man approached in an old sedan from a driveway on Nate's right. *Lots of luck getting in this line*, Nate thought. But then Nate watched himself as he stopped short of the driveway and motioned for the man to get in line in front of him. Without turning around, very visibly, the driver lifted his right arm and waved his thanks. Nate saw the gesture, felt the man's feeling of thanks as something personal and real, and he began to cry. Nate physically felt bitterness, anger, negativity, and anxiety lift like someone had removed weights from his neck and chest and mind.

Nate felt like he was someone other than who he used to be. He didn't have to carry that burden any longer. He was a new person sitting in a new car, and his old truck was gone. The man in the sedan who he'd just helped was just like him. Nate was in a position to help others feel better, the way he needed to feel better. He had that power now.

He realized that The Stranger had been God, or an agent of God. God traded Nate His life for Nate's old, stinky one. Who would do that? (God apparently wasn't very smart.) But Nate wasn't going back. This was one exchange he would keep for the rest of his life.

> But put on the Lord Jesus Christ, and make no provision for the flesh, to gratify its desires.
>   Romans 13:14 (ESV)

Short story

Social Services

I saw Dirk with this little kid. Dirk and I work together in the social services office. The kid was blond and wore his hair swooshed up, long in places and shaved in others, like the hip kids have now, modeled after that white rapper. And he already had an earring. Nine years old, skinny. When the kid walked by with Dirk, it turned everything upside down for me.

Dirk had him. They walked over this way by my desk, and then out the sliding glass door to the outer walkway leading to the parking lot, where they would get in Dirk's car and drive around until a temporary foster situation opened up. The kid was bawlin' his eyes out, stayin' close to Dirk like a little puppy, meek and submissive. That messed with me, and hot tears blurred my vision. Chopped in the gut by the trouble that'd found this kid.

I scooted my chair over to Eduardo's desk. He didn't look up from his typing.

"There's something wrong with me," I told him.

Eduardo turned and lowered his head so he could look at me over his glasses, like he did. He was a tremendously savvy individual. He was afraid if I continued he might have to tell the authorities because he was obligated to tell of crimes or drug abuse among co-workers because we all work with kids. He wasn't happy about listening to what I had to say, afraid of hearin' it, in fact. He liked me, or maybe he just didn't want to have to go through the hassle of breakin' in somebody else.

"Did you see what just happened here?" I asked.

"You mean with Dirk and the niño?"

"Yeah."

"What of it?"

"It's messin' with me, man," I told him, still basically functional, but with stray tears running down my cheeks.

Eduardo looked at me and waited, and the way he did that weakened the dam I depended on to hold back my emotions.

"When that kid and Dirk got over near my desk I literally saw Dirk turn into a big black man. That's how big his heart is."

Eduardo watched me, and glanced from my eyes to the tears and back. He relaxed ever so slightly at hearing that this was not the confession of a crime, that he might not have to report me.

"That little kid's goin' through the ringer. He only cries here, around Dirk, his only safe place," I said, sobs punctuating my sentences, beginning to lose it. "As they were walkin' down the hall, that's when Dirk turned back to Dirk bein' white. You know why he turned back? He should've knelt down and hugged the little

115

guy, let him cry it out. Pain like that has got to get out or it turns a person mean."

Eduardo turned and looked back at his monitor, trying to gather himself to begin typing again, but I saw how glassy his eye was and the moisture starting to pool in the corner. He didn't want to lose it in front of me. Bunch of cryin' men at the DSHS. What would Lilly our boss say?

"God can do anything he wants," I said, crying openly now. "He can take a whole office of crybabies and hold it together, in spite of the budget crunch if He feels like it."

I wasn't makin' much natural sense but Eduardo understood and looked back at me. There was a tear in his other eye too.

"You know why God has this office, has us here? We could be cut tomorrow, but you know why He has us here?"

"Becuz we're helpin' people, helpin' kids," Eduardo said, turning back to his keyboard. He hunted and pecked a few more words onto the request for a restraining order against the little blond guy's dad.

Eduardo was a lousy typer, but he had a good feel this job. He'd been that little kid with Dirk.

A Small Seed

I was sitting in church one Sunday, listening to the sermon, when I got a surprise. Our pastor, to underscore his message with an object lesson, introduced a scene from the movie *Seabiscuit* depicting the first meeting between Seabiscuit's eventual trainer, Tom Smith, and the equine champion's wealthy owner, Charles Howard. I panicked and hurriedly tried to recall the scene before it began playing on the big screen, a "potential-for-public-bawling" alarm blaring in my mind. I tried especially to remember how poignant it was and how much danger I might be in. Although I admired those whose emotional connection with God eclipsed what others thought of them and cried freely in church, as a rule I avoided sobbing myself on the grounds that it made me feel vulnerable (all right, a double standard). This time, there wasn't enough warning; I couldn't recall the scene in time.

The clip played: Howard finds Smith in the bush, coaxing a broken-down, cast- off horse toward healing.

Howard wants to know why Smith is making the effort. "Because I can," says Smith. "You don't throw a whole life away just because it's banged up a little."

Quickly the sentiment about not giving up on the sick horse spread to any being, and in particular, people. This was, of course, the way God felt about everyone on the planet. As the clip finished, I felt His compassion for people I'd known through the years, and people I didn't know, like the homeless and the incarcerated whom I'd judged, who'd had crushing disappointments and trouble. Even if their calamities were of their own doing, God treated them with compassion and gave them healing and a fresh start, just as the trainer did with the sick horse in the movie.

I felt God strongly in that moment. Tears streamed from my eyes and down my cheeks. I brushed them away—I managed to avoid making any noise—thinking that if people saw the tears, they saw them.

Later that evening, in a remarkable coincidence, I noticed *Seabiscuit* on top of a big pile of books destined for sale. I rescued the bestseller and turned to a page at random to see if I remembered the scene, playing with the idea that the book might merit rereading. The print in the inexpensive paperback was so fine and the pictures so ridiculously small that I gave up after a few pages. But my appetite was whetted by reading just that much of Laura Hillenbrand's grand telling of the little horse's improbable, breathtaking climb from bad-tempered also-ran to common person's inspiration, and the gifted team that discovered and reinvented him.

Soon I reserved a larger-print version of the book online, and drove to our local library to fetch it. I joined an Asian woman in a line serviced by two busy clerks, a short man with glasses and wavy hair and a tall woman with long, blond locks. An African-American girl who appeared to be about 12, her arms full of books, got in line behind me. The plain black frames of her glasses, her armload of reading material, and quiet manner gave her a shy, studious air.

I looked away from the desk and librarians, my mind pondering various indescribable things—I often forgot what I was thinking—and when I looked back, a focused, fortyish Caucasian male had inserted himself behind one of the patrons currently talking with a clerk, in effect making himself the first person in a new, closer line. Irritated, I weighed the discomfort and effort a confrontation would require against a longer wait time. Weakening my position was the thought that maybe the library recognized two lines; what did I know?

A few minutes later, I was the next person in line. The patron to the right finished checking out and Johnny-come-lately moved quickly toward the available librarian in my place.

"I'm sorry, sir, there's only one line," she said to him courteously. Looking toward me, she asked, "May I help you?"

Yes! In yo' face, guy who cut in line!

Exasperated, the man backed away from the desk and moved toward the line I'd just stood in. "Thank you," I said as I walked toward her, "I didn't know if I should tell him that or not." I gave her my card and she scanned it and left to retrieve my book from the "hold" section. I looked over my shoulder and noticed that, unbelievably, the line-cutter had moved only a few feet back and stood beside the young black girl, instead of getting in line behind her. I knew she'd been waiting longer than he had. Taking advantage of my clerk's absence, I walked over to him. Looking in his eyes, I said clearly, "She's next," and nodded toward the girl. I looked back at him. He nodded once slowly to signify he understood, the speed of the movement contrasting with the visible anger flaring in his dark eyes. I was aware of my accelerated breathing and heart rate as I returned to the clerks' desk. Confronting the man on behalf of the child was easier than doing it just for me.

The male librarian finished with his customer and asked the next person to come forward. Too loud behind me I heard the man say to the little girl, "Go ahead!" It was unnecessary and rude. She brought her armload of treasure to the checkout desk and set it down.

The female clerk returned with my book and I checked it out. As I opened the door to leave, the girl appeared behind me, her arms still full of books, and I was happy to hold the door for her. "Thank you," she said quietly, and walked out into the parking lot. I wondered if she had said it for two reasons.

"You're welcome," I said lightly. I didn't walk with her going toward my car because I didn't want her to feel like she owed me anything.

No one saw the old white guy stand up to the fellow who cut in line, except the little girl. Even though she might not tell anyone about it, perhaps that gesture would help, in a small way, to bridge the significant distance between races. That gap didn't seem to be diminishing, but I was waiting on God because I knew He wanted to bring us together into one body. God, help us to take it to the streets—or to the library.

Memoir

Heralds of
the Lord Most High

A n event loomed. I was working 40 hours a week
at the time, with a 40-minute commute by bus
both morning and evening, and I had a number of
extracurricular activities going on. The day of the event
I wondered if I had spread myself too thin.

It was an evening of prayer for a woman and her husband on a yearlong mission trip to Africa. The woman's
parents were family friends of ours, and they organized
the gathering. Our friends had been missionaries in
Papua New Guinea. Out of love for their daughter and
her husband, and knowing the significant spiritual and
natural challenges their daughter and her husband faced
from their own experience, they wanted to help.

My wife and I had committed to going to the prayer
time. I don't particularly remember how work went the
day of the event, but I do know that as we drove the
significant distance to the house where the gathering
was to take place that evening, I felt that I had made a

mistake. We decided to avoid paying the (at the time) brand new toll on the 520 bridge, and drove around Lake Washington. We got caught in heavy traffic. We didn't have enough time to begin with, and as we sat through cycles of lights without moving, I tried to avoid looking at the clock on the dashboard. It seemed like every time I glanced over, several more minutes had ticked by. It was torture, sitting there in the enclosed space with the clock in my field of vision. I imagined trooping into the meeting late, to the irritation of all present.

As often happens before we attend a spiritual event, my wife and I were short with one another; just being civil took superhuman effort. I confess that I wasn't particularly pleasant during our ride over. There was a palpable heaviness in the air, evidenced by the snarled traffic and the dark, windy, rain-drenched night, and it was also apparent in our strained emotions. I regretted this trip. I wanted to turn around and head home. Searing thoughts burned through my mind: *How are you going to make it in to work tomorrow? You're trying to do too much. You're going to burn out; then what good will you be? This is just your ego trying to make a good showing. The people at this meeting don't even like you; they tolerate you because they have to. God makes them because they're Christians, but you have nothing to add. Do you really think your prayers are going to help some people all the way over in Africa? You're going to be so late you might as well not even go; you'll just burden the others.*

I felt small and futile and only continued driving out of stubbornness, resignation, and momentum.

It took us over an hour to drive to Duvall, a small town to the northeast of Seattle. We were, of course, appreciably late. We knocked on the door, and the host came to let us in. It didn't appear as though they had started praying yet. Thank God for that.

The host couple lived in a spacious house. People were in the kitchen and dining area, and were filing into the living room to sit down. Some brought beverages. Two dogs—a black one named Skippy that looked like it was part Labrador and maybe Australian shepherd, and a good-natured golden retriever named Honey—mingled among the assembly, trying to gauge the strangers' makeup and mood. A young couple's 15-month-old daughter wobbled on unsteady legs that belied her spunk and precociousness. She was outrageously cute in her innocence, curiosity, and wonder, with two short pigtails angling up from her round head in a lighthearted satire of the devil's horns.

As we began praying, a valve released in my overwrought psyche and I heard God's calming influence enter through these people's voices, each prayer adding a significant and meaningful part to the orchestra ascending to God on high. In turn, I added my voice. The Bible says that these prayers do help their subjects; I began to believe it and feel it.

Despite the now-peaceful environment and the bonhomie of fellowship, an idea came to me. This seemed to be my lot, and I was a loner in this it seemed: I wanted to bind some spirits. The question was, was it of the Lord? That was the difficulty. There's no way to tell. One had an unction—and I thought of this a lot, this phenomenon—and there was no way to tell if it was of the Lord until one did it and saw what happened. Even then, feedback didn't always indicate whether it was or wasn't God. All one could do was try, and leave the results to God.

The Bible and Christian experience say different things about this. The problem was that sometimes these thoughts or ideas I got were not easily dismissed; they worked on me.

Venturing out would be risky. The great, blessed space that we had come to presently, in light of the evening's rocky start, was at stake. Sometimes it just wasn't in the Spirit's mind to start binding spirits when the general tenor of the evening prayers spoke of a focus on God and His goodness and power. I didn't want to invoke this bent into the gentle gathering because of some Pentecostal formula or pattern. It hadn't been on my agenda to do so; the thought had simply appeared in my mind.

Finally, I decided that I wasn't content with the way things were. "In Jesus' name I bind a spirit of oppression and trouble in this couple's midst." I went on like that for a bit, praying for our friends' daughter and son-in-law in Africa as though I were there, feeling the oppression (which maybe I was, a bit). "According to the scripture we submit ourselves to God and resist you Satan in the power of God for our brother and sister overseas." Then I quoted Jesus: "Behold I give you power, to tread upon serpents and scorpions, and over all the power of the enemy, and nothing shall by any means hurt you." As I spoke, I kept my eyes closed. I felt tense, and worried I had ruined the evening by introducing and exercising this strident aspect of prayer into an otherwise calm evening. I finished my prayer.

With my eyes still closed, I felt the golden retriever's warm, soft, and clean fur brushing against the front of my legs as she sought affection. It was the gentlest, friendliest sensation I can remember.

I opened my eyes. I saw the upturned face of the toddler gazing into my eyes, in full acceptance and without fear of me, like, *Right on, dude!* or an Austin Powers-like *Yeah baby!* She seemed to be in total agreement with what I had done, standing maybe a foot away, her pacifier sticking jauntily out of her mouth, momentarily forgotten in light of beholding this large and unusual but apparently savvy being. She hadn't been in the room when I began to pray. Her little face, seemingly large because it encompassed my entire field of view, was at once innocence and knowledge, and in one accord with the Lord. We were on the same page, allies in a monumental and ageless struggle against the enemy of our King. God includes babies in his plan. Matthew 21:16 says: "You have taught children and infants to give you praise" (NLT), and Psalm 127:5 adds, "[young children] shall speak with their enemies in the gate." God actually uses the vulnerability, spontaneity, and innocence of children to confound the devil's devious ways.

The dog and the baby seemed to be of the same spirit, stepping in to comfort and encourage me after my gambit, two loving witnesses that not only confirmed my presence in the gathering, but my prayers against the enemy.

It was a great evening. I recall a young preacher saying one night long ago, "If you can stand the stretch, God will pull you through."

Yes He will. Hallowed be His Name.

Short story

Dear Krusto

W e would like to welcome you to Earth for the 2012 Summer Olympics. Being from the planet Talaxo, you may not be familiar with customs here on Earth. You have expressed a keen interest in learning the history and mechanics of the games so that you might better understand what you are watching. I'll be glad to explain things to you.

First, forget about history. The games started in ancient Greece and then were not held at all for many centuries. In 1896, the Greeks, led by Pierre de Coubertain, a Frenchman and founder of the International Olympic Committee (IOC), successfully revived the games, and we have held them every four years since. But if you try to frame what you are seeing in a historical context, you will only confuse yourself. As we say here on Earth, *Forget about it!* In fact, don't just dismiss the ancient history of the games—ignore their more-recent history too. It will be a lot easier if we just think about the 2012 games in isolation.

Krusto, my friend, you have to understand that you have been watching only a fraction of the events actually taking place now in London. This is because you are watching during the day, in what we call "prime time." NBC has to be judicious about the events they choose to show. That's the television network that broadcasts the Olympics, by the way. Rival networks might show something that would threaten to draw even hardcore Olympics fans away from the games: a soap opera or game show by day, a cunning reality series or bawdy sitcom by night. Each NBC Olympics telecast has to pack considerable commercial wallop to compete with these juggernauts. TV is a business, and TV programming must be extremely appealing, even enchanting. (I do concede that TV must very occasionally pose as an impartial communicator of information and events.)

Programs must be so compelling that viewers will happily sit through commercials to see the show. This is essential. All decisions about TV programming are calculated from the perspective of making money; this focus on money does not lapse for even a nanosecond.

Krusto, because you are an alien, you might not fully understand what I'm about to tell you. Here on Earth, sex is a big deal. Thinking about sex motivates people, big time. Between couples in private, sex often lacks pizzazz and frequency, but on TV and in the movies and even on the radio, sex takes on surreal proportions. When it comes to TV commercials, the content is 99% sex and 1% humor, which is often sexual anyway. Marketers hire sexually attractive women to help sell everything from dish soap to minivans. The product does not necessarily have to relate to the female body to effectively harness the power of sex in a sales pitch. On the contrary. The best and most successful advertising campaigns result when the product and sex have no connection at all, like in commercials for food, baby diapers, or even farm equipment. Everyone accepts—even expects—that sex will be introduced at any time and in any context. Advertisements without racy visuals and innuendo make viewers antsy; they sense that something is fundamentally wrong.

Advertising is only half of the matter. Television executives saturate programming with sex to ensure that it has a chance of lasting for longer than one episode. Even children's cartoons have female characters with grossly over-emphasized sexual anatomy. This not only helps to mature children rapidly, it also entertains adult viewers, particularly fathers who may occasionally have to spend time watching television with their children. Dads often plop the kids down in front of the screen while they do more important things like look at stuff on the Internet, but if they *have* to be with their children, they might as well get something for it.

Krusto, you also need to understand that until very recently, women were marginalized here on Earth. To some extent, they still are, but in certain places, they have obtained more freedom and respect. The Olympic Games functions as a celebration of all the gains women have made. In 1896 there were just a handful of women competing in the games. Now, fully 40 percent of the thousands of athletes at the Olympics are women, and even countries whose governments have repressed women's rights are beginning to send a few women to compete, though unfortunately they are dressed in modest uniforms. This attire is disheartening to liberal countries like the United States, but at least women from these other nations are allowed to compete in the games. One hopes that these anachronistic governments will abandon their modesty when they see their athletes rubbing shoulders with provocative, liberated, well-endowed women from more enlightened countries.

You're asking me why nearly every time you turn the games on, you see women's beach volleyball. That's a good question, especially because beach volleyball is a relatively new sport at the Olympics. Remember what I told you, though: Forget history, and consider TV programming fundamentals. NBC is not interested in reaching an audience that appreciates traditional athletic competitions. Those are boring to watch.

It is also helpful to think of it this way: The Olympic Games are not for athletes; they are for spectators. The tailor-made event for spectators, Krusto, is women's beach volleyball.

You ask how women can progress as people and athletes if they are simply regarded as sex objects. It's a good question, my friend. A few very radical women bring up the same point, in fact, but no one pays any attention. Too much money and political power are involved.

Really, what is wrong with this little game in the sand with attractive, young and near-nude women? Don't forget, the Olympics is also a chance to display your patriotism! Married, middle-aged men can sit on the couch and lust to their hearts' content even if the wife is present, all in the name of national loyalty. Go Misty! Go Kerri! Good spike! Nice dig! Go USA!

Women athletes must be in good shape to play beach volleyball, so overweight women won't be playing. Furthermore, Olympic and FCC rules allow the athletes to wear the tiniest bikinis, which grow less encumbering, as do all rules about modesty, as time progresses. Male beach volleyball players wear shirts, modest trunks, and hats, but then they have much lower viewer ratings. Not hard to see the connection there. In just one sport, you have extreme sex appeal and an event that shines the spotlight on female athletes. Women may make up less than half of Olympic Games participants, but thanks to beach volleyball, a disproportionately large amount of TV broadcast time features women's events. This is a huge gain for women.

You really are something of a prude, Krusto! You point out that some countries are just beginning to send female athletes at all, and that these and several other nations have higher standards of modesty than those displayed in beach volleyball. Furthermore, you say that the United States and other countries seem to be flouting their sexuality despite the objections and offense taken by these other nations. Dear Krusto, everyone knows that the United States is the world's cultural and political innovator. And what of this anomaly: How could a modestly attired team be allowed to triumph over a bikini-clad team? Or what if two teams with modest apparel competed in the championship? This could adversely affect viewership, and hurt the sponsors. NBC can't have it.

I have some good news for you, Krusto. Beer companies and other likeminded businesses proposed an idea to the IOC that the Committee considered, adopted, and enthusiastically implemented. In 2016, to really reconnect us to Olympic history and tradition, to advance the cause of women's athletics, and to add a powerful spectator draw that will only benefit the other, less popular Olympic events, the IOC has declared that no media coverage of any men's or women's events may begin without first showing a full hour of nude female Greco-Roman mud wrestling. That's still four years away, but the tickets are already sold out. (I know I got mine, baby!) The United States is taking the lead on this, and has already hired a coach and found 80 young women aspirants, all recruited via *The Jerry Springer Show*.

Those 80 will be culled to a sleek squad of babes, um, female athletes, boasting the best balance of sex appeal, er, physical gifts, and appearance of athletic prowess. The US government has volunteered to send helper teams and seed money to backward countries so that they will have their teams trained and ready to compete in time. For stubborn countries that hesitate, there will be powerful economic incentives (spelled "sanctions") to force them on board. By 2020, no country will be allowed to participate in the Olympics in either men's or women's events unless they send representatives to the mud wrestling event. And as time goes on, the more traditional sports will drop out altogether and be replaced with more modern, pertinent competitions.

Are you beginning to feel the Olympic spirit, my alien friend?

Shawn

We were walking through the halls of his hotel, the gazelle and I. He was trying to lobby me, as he sometimes did.

"Say man, you should come over tomorrow night. I've got my lady coming over, and she could bring her friend. Just try it out. No tellin' what we might get into…"

He probably said this both because he remained perennially hopeful I would not dismiss his proposal—he certainly wouldn't in my place—and he knew it was a slight barb to me, a kind of riling up and testing of others that seemed to be in his nature. And it did aggravate me. He knew I was married. Shawn was different from me, probably fundamentally different in this way, maybe others as well.

Shawn and I had been friends for a long time. He was 28 and I was 32. He was black and I was white. I'd known him a long time before he stepped (surprisingly) into his present celebrity.

We'd met in study hall—all right, detention—in high school. I was there for skipping class, and he was in trouble for something else, I forget what. Despite our age difference, I was only one grade ahead of him. I had missed a couple years because I got pretty sick for a while. But I was healthy now; God had taken his time about it, but healed me nonetheless.

I forget how we connected. It wasn't because of sports; he was an athlete and I could barely walk in a straight line. Maybe it was like that old movie, *The Defiant Ones*, where a black and a white criminal escaped prison handcuffed together. Only we were forged together by some unusual link that nobody saw or knew about, but just as surely held us together, yoked escapees, brothers. As I could with a number of people, I seemed to be able to see the whole Shawn, his gentleness and dignity and simplicity. As the Bible says, a man without guile. I saw character deficiencies and even some bad in him, but couldn't help but like him anyway. At times I felt a little guilty about this, and thought it was a weakness in my character. Other times I saw it as a gift from God, to be able to see people like that, looking beyond their faults, perhaps like how God saw them. With God, loving someone never stemmed from a lack of character.

"I can't do it, man. You know that," I said. He looked back at me as he walked through the posh hotel, and I met his gaze. Involuntarily I smiled thinly and raised my eyebrows a bit. He looked away, a hard distracted look etched on his face. He probably thought that he really didn't know me, wondered why we were friends.

He wanted to share with me in this realm also, like he probably did with some of his teammates.

I thought I heard, "Gettin' religious on me again." I wasn't sure. More words like that seemed to float back to me as we made our way to the lobby of the fancy hotel where celebrities, wanna-be celebrities, celebrity hangers-on, and maybe the occasional normal person stayed.

My morals probably made him question his relationships with the opposite sex, and sensitized his conscience. Maybe they made him think about his mother, and consider that her stance on these things was like mine. She would be disappointed that he didn't sympathize more with her, and remember how much his dad hurt *her* with *his* running around. Maybe he still hung out with me (increasingly rare meetings on account of his career) because I reminded him of his mother. She had "gotten religion" a long time before I had and was influential in my change of heart and mind, which began during the illness that caused me to be held back in school.

*   *   *

That illness is the bane and foundation of my life. While I was sick, I didn't hate God, but I disliked Him. And I thought He was either not all-powerful, or somehow clueless, or worse, unconcerned about His creation, and especially, disinterested in *me*. It made me question the notion of God's love, how He, having all power, just didn't seem to be bothered about stuff that hurt me. I wondered if He simply existed on some plane that I wasn't connected with. Without having gone through that illness, though, I would have navigated life lost and rudderless. I can honestly say that it developed character in me. The rub about character is that there just doesn't seem any easy way to get it. Now I can see God's love in allowing the illness, how it made me get serious about my faith, and about life, and how I am grateful now for the smallest things. I take very little for granted. And when someone gives me something—what I might have taken for granted before—I recognize it and thank them. I am amazed at how selfish and arrogant I was before. I am not perfect now, that's for sure, but without that trial, I would have been a sad case, a waste of a human being.

*   *   *

Shawn's high school and collegiate athletic careers were not stellar, especially in light of where he was now. He was a tight end back then, and didn't look much like a football player because he wasn't that big, or at least didn't appear imposing compared to the giant linemen he huddled with. But up close Shawn was not built like me at all. He was solid, with a wide chest and sinewy arms and legs. He moved easily and deliberately, his flesh seemingly radiating energy. I have to admit that there was just something stable and good about him, even though it was tough to see during our conversation in the hotel.

Like always, though, he would work through it, move on and end up liking me again. Or so I thought at the time. We were friends before he became rich and famous, and there were precious few of his old buddies who did not expect to share in his largesse. I can honestly say that I didn't want his money or the prestige from being seen with him, which worked well, because he didn't seem especially eager to show me off as his friend. I wasn't bothered. My prolonged illness turned me reclusive then, and I never quite recovered my ability to socialize.

We did share a few long distance calls a month, and he always sent me tickets to his home games when he played for Philadelphia. After the games, we would get together. Sometimes my tickets arrived by courier just a day before the game. Once, I got tickets three hours before kickoff. But I was always pretty sure they would come, and looked forward to the games. I wondered why he didn't just get me season tickets, but this was classic Shawn. He liked to do things on the spur of the moment, even if there were a whole series of moments when he always reacted the same way. He struggled with commitment and liked to keep his options open.

To Shawn, including me in his world—and I was quite distinct from everyone else in it—was probably like some ritual of honor he felt bound to, since his mom died, a way of keeping her presence in his life while giving him something to hang on to from his former foundations, which were tested daily in the chaotic world of professional football.

He turned into an alcove off the hall. I remember this setting well, a small anteroom with no windows and a little couch along the wall. The room isolated us together for a few moments. There was an attractive sensation of peace here that I felt despite the earlier tension between us, the kind of place where if I were alone I could sit down and rest a minute before picking up my cares and continuing my day. Shawn was standing with his back to one of the soft-toned, beige walls, facing me, a bit obliquely. He was irritated. He just couldn't seem to relate to me in this area of life—women—and it frustrated him. He and his teammates had a natural, unspoken camaraderie about this, a bond that he was accustomed to, and he couldn't quite decipher our relationship without this primary key.

I vividly remember what happened next because it was unusual for me. I walked toward him and put my hand on his left arm, the one closest to me, and looked into his eyes. At first he wouldn't look at me.

"Shawn, I have this great fear that you and lots of other guys are going to go through life without ever having made love." I could tell what I said startled him.

My lack of discomfort in moving toward him and saying this surprised me. But a great welling emotion in my chest made it easy and natural. The Lord moved me like this occasionally.

"You're missing something. God's best in sex is for folks who make a commitment to each other. Without that it's never going to be completely satisfying." When he finally looked at me, I could see my words had registered.

The next time the Eagles played at home, I didn't get tickets. It hurt, but I felt peace that mitigated the sting. The Lord willed me to speak to him that day, and I would just have to accept the consequences. I could no more have refrained from saying it than I could refuse a free ticket to Heaven.

I didn't think of Shawn as much without the periodic football tickets to remind me. When I did, old slew foot tried to make me question what I'd said to him at the hotel, but I knew that God had spoken through me, devil may care.

A year slipped by. I went out to the mailbox to retrieve our mail one day, and I returned to a warm room in the small home I shared with my wife of ten years to read it. An ornate envelope lay among the regular pieces of mail; I figured it was a credit card offer. But I opened it, and was pleasantly astounded to find an invitation to Shawn's upcoming wedding.

Eventually, skepticism crept in: Given his dalliances over the years, how well could this end? But the feeling passed; I forced that lack of faith, that judgmental attitude, that fear of new things and new relationships to vanish.

I had seen plenty of evidence demonstrating that when someone takes a step of faith like marriage, even if they don't have their life together in other ways, God makes up for what's lacking and honors the commitment. It doesn't have so much to do with the person as it does with God.

At the wedding, I could see that Shawn had changed. He didn't look at the pretty girls like he used to, and he seemed to be more peaceful and settled. During the reception, he found me and walked up to me deliberately. "Thank you so much for saying what you did to me that day in the hotel," he said. "I was mad for weeks, but the truth has a way of sinking in. And I apologize to you, because even after I accepted the truth of what you said, I was too proud to confess it to you." Sometimes people speak softly and powerfully like this, and my eyes mist up. My heart expanded.

He went on. "I'm scared as hell right now, but I know I'm doing the right thing. Maybe God will help me in spite of myself." He smiled. "I tried to get too much from too many women, and didn't realize that the greedier I got, the less I had. It's humbling to make this change, but I have peace, and that's worth a plenty. And I love that little gal," he said, looking over at his bride as she chatted amicably with their family and friends.

Vignette

Touched by an Angel

I t feels as though I often begin a story by saying how hard my life is. Well, during the timeframe of this story, it reached unprecedented levels. I was like Job, and God had given Satan more access to me. Why would He do that? Probably because He wanted to build my faith and character.

Neither was the Lord answering my prayers for help.

I finished a particularly trying two days at work. I was just barely holding on to my job at the Census Bureau as an information technology clerk. Part of my work problems might have related to the particular lanyard I chose to wear around my neck that held my security badge and ID. Woven into the red material of the lanyard in big white letters, it proclaimed "I (heart) Jesus."

It was unclear how pertinent to my job troubles this lanyard was, but a brother on the job who was Presbyterian, as he looked upon it askance, remarked, "There's an awful big responsibility on you in wearing

142

that here." I agreed—and I thought to myself *I must be crazy to wear this, I am not worthy*—but I had prayed about it and it had seemed as though God said to wear it. Then I was trapped; after wearing it there a few days, I didn't want to back down.

The accumulated job stress, trouble sleeping, family responsibilities, and other difficult circumstances reached a crescendo late one Thursday night. That night I had had trouble sleeping, as usual. I drifted off around 11 PM, and about a half hour later, the neighbor's car alarm went off, waking me. Once I awake at night after being asleep for a while—no matter how short the duration is—it is difficult to go back to sleep. I had slept only a half hour. It was possible I would not sleep any more, or for hours, which was almost as bad, before having to start my next day. I later imagined Satan lifting his wand and inspiring a human dupe to trigger the car alarm. The impression was strong and sinister.

My ability to handle stress is hard enough when I get enough rest.

I began to pray to the Lord on my knees beside the bed. I moaned, "I'm the guy who can't get enough sleep. I'm the guy who is bothered by Janice [one of my wife's friends who scares me with her controlling tendencies]. I'm the guy who… [some other failure or fear]." Each sentence began this way, and I wept in desperation. I imagined losing my job. Adding to my pain was that I saw myself as one who, for the past month, had not been able to hear from God through sermons, His Word, other believers, or in his own spirit as he normally could.

Eventually I was exhausted, and because praying didn't seem to be helping, I got back in bed. I don't know if I drifted off or was awake and quiet for a while, but at about two in the morning, I became conscious of the Lord's presence in my room. I was not at all afraid, or anxious, and I felt peace and energy. I was not worried about work the next day, or that I should be sleeping. The positive change in me was surely God answering my prayer.

Then God told me that I was a mighty man of valor. I answered, "No, I'm not, I'm afraid and anxious." God countered, "Don't forget about your trip to the Philippines." It had been a long time since I recalled a mission to the Philippines that my wife and I had taken several years earlier, but I had to agree that during the 11 days of the trip, I had been brave in spirit and God did miracles through and for me. It was His work, really, but I cooperated with what I believed He wanted me to do, which I struggled with back in the states: I am sometimes cowed at church about speaking publicly the words of prophecy and encouragement I receive, or describing visions I've seen.

There is God's perspective and then there is the worldly perspective. It's better if by God's grace and help we can see things from His perspective, not what we think His perspective is, but a revelation of it. That night God revealed that He thinks I am brave.

Then God pointed me to Psalm 34.

It was amazing how I could appropriate for myself assurances from this psalm that just a couple of hours earlier seemed unattainable. I attributed this to God's spirit that had come into my room. I want to pass on something in particular.

Earlier in the week, mostly subconsciously, I had been struggling with the thought—an accusation really—that my relationship with the Lord was off. I had a relationship, for sure, but something had happened to skew it, and I felt that it was probably something I had done, or a wrong attitude I carried. I do know that I had been reading a book on spiritual warfare that said something like the following: "Most Christians engage in spiritual warfare just so they can live a more normal life." The book seemed to insinuate that this was wrong, perhaps even sinful, and that spirit warfare was for helping others and expanding God's kingdom. The author, or my interpretation of what the author said (which might have been wrong), or something else I wasn't aware of (for example Satan), accused me of being selfish.

I had to admit that I wanted a life: health for my family and me, enough sustenance, and a family and friends. I even wanted the abundant life that Jesus promised His followers, which in my opinion can include material things with the spiritual, emotional, and psychical. I felt guilty for wanting those things. The article's author may have even implied that a spiritual person should not even pray for relief from suffering. By making a commitment for Christ, I know I have signed up for suffering. But I don't believe it's wrong to pray to be healthy and pain free.

Psalm 34 agreed with me.

These verses revealed to me the subconscious issues with which I had been wrestling, and freed me from them:

> ¹² *Who is the man who desires life,*
>   *And loves many days, that he may see good?*
> ¹³ *Keep your tongue from evil,*
>   *And your lips from speaking deceit.*
> ¹⁴ *Depart from evil and do good;*
>   *Seek peace and pursue it.*

That would be me who desires life and loves many days. God was saying that it's OK to want to see and experience good in this life. (And to receive the gift, one should be honest and do the right thing.) The psalm liberated me. It said that I could be me and still please God.

The psalm continues:

> ¹⁸ *The LORD is near to those who have a broken heart,*
>   *And saves such as have a contrite spirit.*

When I was crying and troubled by my bed, the Lord heard me, and answered me with His word (the psalm). These lines follow:

> ¹⁹ *Many are the afflictions of the righteous,*
>   *But the LORD delivers him out of them all.*

This verse was helpful in two ways. It let me know that those who are righteous—righteous only by believing in Jesus, not by works that one does—should expect suffering. In a sense, suffering signifies God's approval of those who suffer. Secondly, it promises that God will rescue them from every trouble, in His time.

That experience of peace, clarity, and emotional reassurance lasted through the night and into the next day and the next. May the change that God did for and in me that night continue. The works of the mighty King shall endure.

His Old Man
Really Loved Him

He'd been dreaming about his dear son. As he woke, the moment of hope and freedom that he was experiencing at the end of the dream flickered out, replaced by an appalling, unfamiliar oppression, a feeling of separation from his son that overwhelmed and panicked him. It occurred to him that this was the day he'd awaited and dreaded for what seemed like eons, and now it was here and there was no going back.

This would surely be the hardest day of his life, but it was of utmost importance that it take place. He wasn't ready. He would never be ready.

He'd been in favor of his son joining the service; one might even say it had been his idea. Last night he'd received word that his son had been taken prisoner, and was now in enemy hands. They would torture and try to break him, but he knew his son had the stuff.

A deeply painful stroke smacked him mid-torso, real and raw, springing from the place where the enemy dwelt, the dim shadows of the dark and alien realm underpinning the world of men.

He crossed over to the couch and sat down slowly, holding his stomach. It had begun. Had this been a good idea, his son going? It had seemed right. He glanced down and saw that his socks were worn and soiled, there on his feet. The sight made little impression; his mind and feelings were focused entirely on his dear boy. He continued to sit on the sofa. Outside of torment's enclosure momentarily, he felt his socks rub against the skin on his lower legs and feet. He had wished from the beginning that he could have gone in his son's stead, but that had been ruled out by certain ungainly arrangements.

As Romans hammered spikes into Jesus's hands and feet to pin Him to a plank and drag Him up into the shocked firmament, the old man lost his composure, jumped up and struck the wall with his fist so hard the ground around Jerusalem rocked. Angry tears sprung from his eyes, and he collapsed onto the couch.

A perceptive aide quickly detached himself from his regiment and ran to the old man.

"Do you want to change the plan, Sir?" the aide asked. He had been afraid to voice the question, and more afraid not to. He peered intently at his general, but the old man did not turn. He seemed not to have heard the question and did not answer. As the aide carefully withdrew, he noticed blood intermingling with the old man's tears, swatches of crimson soaking the back of the general's shirt and pants.

When the old man simply could not tolerate the excruciating pain any longer, he hammered a nearby wall with his bare knuckles, and the veil of the temple split in two. Serpents of lightning snaked across the dark night sky, to resounding peels of deafening thunder. To steady himself, to remind himself that it would be thus for his son soon and very soon, he gave word to his men to release captive Old Testament believers. As they rose from their graves, they walked clumsily, like drunken people, and those who saw them marveled and were afraid.

The diversion helped, but his heart and attention soon returned to his son. This part of their plan required that the old man ignore his son's calamity, and let him proceed alone. Those in his son's retinue—even hand-picked men who had become his friends—were unable to help him. Certain women his son had befriended, their tender hearts anyway, would comfort his son more than his chosen men. The old man determined to extend lavish love and forgiveness to Peter, to not hold anything against any of his son's associates, or anyone else. This would be difficult, but he would surely grant his son's dying request, for his son's sake alone.

Again, at his very core, he asked himself if sending his son to his death had been wise. It was costing too much. Together with his son, and his and his son's Friend, he had counted the cost beforehand, but in practice, the crucifixion pained him more than he could stand. He could still stop it. He would suffer loss, but his son would be restored to him immediately. All risk would cease. His son was much more valuable to him than the souls they wanted to win.

In an impulsive moment of indescribable and extravagant love that came from his deepest being, the old man had offered everything he had to the world of men: Now that matters were immeasurably difficult and painful, would he repent, change his mind? No. It wasn't like him. They had made the plan, and he would not abandon it now. But if he let his son go through with this, would any understand, would any turn?

As the old man pondered this question, he realized that if the cross changed even one person, it was worth the cost. He hunkered down and waited for Sunday. There would be no sleep, but rest was irrelevant. As he pulled the socks off his feet and threw them carelessly against a wall, he knew that humans would call this coming Sunday "Easter." In coming centuries, more would attend church this day than at any other time of the year, except for perhaps the arbitrary day that people on the earth chose to celebrate his son's birth.

The spirit was game, and could operate; the old man and his son had confidence in their longtime Friend. The old man looked ahead and glimpsed what appeared to be specks of gold in faraway Sunday services, and elsewhere.

For through Him we both have access by one Spirit to the Father.

Ephesians 2:18

Short story

First Light

Yevgeny Pavlovich drove his white 2004 Cadillac Deville along an empty arterial in Renton, Washington, a subordinate city of Seattle that, to some, fell significantly short of its more esteemed neighbor because it was provincial and lacked vision.

The Caddy was a nice car. Driving it publicly was at once comfortable and provided him with a sense of productivity that was lacking at home.

He paid little attention to a small, decaying strip mall on the right as he passed, but a few blocks beyond, he saw a man at a bus stop turn, affording Pavlovich a clear look at his face.

Pavlovich had seen the man before, or at least his picture. He turned right at the next cross street and pulled his muted, powerful automobile to the curb along a slightly uphill street by an expanse of tall grass dotted with islands of trash and grey, crumbling concrete blocks. He looked up and saw rundown houses and decades-old apartment buildings with South Sea

Island names like Lanai Hi and Aloha Oe. Small white, sharp, reflective stones embedded in drab concrete failed to add glitz to the 1960s buildings. Pavlovich could not place the man. Out of habit, he turned off the ignition to save gas and sat in the residual warmth of the posh car.

In the last few years, it had been difficult for Pavlovich to recall things that once came easily, as he once had no trouble doing—in fact had zeal and a talent for—in his youth. His weakening memory worried him considerably, so he taught himself not to think about it, like not touching a sore. He discovered over time a bonus for this systematic avoidance: In a span of minutes or hours, sometimes days, he remembered the tidbit, which populated his mind while it was otherwise occupied. This reward weakened his work ethic, however.

Sitting in his car on an unfamiliar road, he was curious who this man might be. His present surroundings did not depress him, as they might have some Americans; they reminded him of home. He inserted a Ne Zhurys cassette tape into his car's player and the dated Ukrainian pop group's music filled the car. As he listened, and as he had hoped, the name of the man who had been standing at the bus stop came to him: Claudio Estrella. Pavlovich also recalled that he was wanted, though by whom he did not know. At this point, his curiosity became mercenary. *Can present scenario perhaps be turned for profit?*

Pavlovich retrieved his cell phone from the pocket of his thin leather jacket and dialed the secret number of a clearinghouse for criminal information. A woman asked for his identification, which he supplied. She asked how she could help him, and he asked for information about Claudio Estrella. After a pause, she explained that Estrella's former cartel was offering 100,000 US dollars for information leading to his capture, or $200,000 for a bona fide proof of kill.

The higher number would go much further in paying Pavlovich's debts, and he owed money to the kind of men who forcefully recouped their loans. For those reasons he was about to opt for the work that paid better, but then had a strong impression to take the job that paid less. The way the impression appeared in his mind was like what happened with forgotten information.

As he verbally committed to the job that paid less, he silently accused himself of getting soft. The woman told Pavlovich he would be contacted soon with the details of his impending meeting with cartel representatives. As he put the phone back in his jacket pocket, the word *peligro* came to mind. He did not know much Spanish, but he knew this word meant "danger." Again he wondered why words and ideas he had forgotten seemingly entered his head from another dimension. They didn't come from him, and although simple, they often appeared more profound than his own ideas. He was learning to consider them, trusting them at times. It seemed like an easier way to live, as if someone else was doing the heavy lifting.

Several minutes after hanging up, he experienced a palpable feeling of relief with the realization that he wouldn't have to kill anyone. He had made a decision based on an impression, and only now did he realize its practical implications.

Pavlovich waited another five minutes and heard the pulsing disco ringtone of his cell. The tone inspired shadowy pictures of a land Pavlovich inhabited 30 years ago, before the dissolution of the Union of Soviet Socialist Republics. He had needed technical support from his cell phone company to get the ringtone to work. Disco was resurfacing in the United States, so he reasoned that from an intelligence standpoint, the ringtone would not draw attention, though actually his unusual appearance, age, and the ringtone's foreign flavor might.

"Hello," he spoke into the phone, incapable as usual of disguising his accent. He had developed the habit of saying "hello" rather than grunting *da* into the receiver, as he had for decades in the former Soviet Union. The enormous effort to affect this small change unfortunately did little to disguise his origins from listeners. But he was oblivious to it. He perceived his speech only from his perspective, at the exertions he had made, rather than garnering information from external sources as to its efficacy.

"Listen, do not speak," a male voice on the phone said in unaccented English. The efficient, detached voice continued, "Go to SeaTac airport tomorrow, Wednesday, at 8:00 AM. Go to the seating area between Starbucks and the DVD shop. It is in the insecure part of the airport just east of Delta Airlines." The man gave the passphrases that Pavlovich and his contact would use to establish identity during the initial part of the meeting. Finally, the voice expediently repeated all of the instructions and asked if Pavlovich understood.

"Yes," he grunted. Immediately the line went dead.

The voice did not name the man he was to meet, nor did it mention Estrella. Pavlovich was not surprised. He guessed the speaker was a subordinate who could not be linked to the powerful cartel officers if he were overheard or caught. Pavlovich reasoned that, because he was not intending to travel himself, and therefore would not be authorized to pass through security, the meeting would take place in the insecure part of the airport out of necessity. Because the man would have just disembarked and passed out of the secure part of the airport, Pavlovich figured he would be unarmed. This was safer for Pavlovich, and the Ukrainian relaxed, knowing he would not need to hire any help or share any of the job's profits.

The rush to find Estrella and the big money bolstered Pavlovich's suspicion that Estrella was dangerous to the cartel. Had he stolen money? They would make an example of him. Might he share information with police agencies or other cartels? They would silence him. Was Estrella trying to create his own brand to rob business from his cartel? They would torture and kill him and his family. Powerful cartel leaders were strongly and unusually motivated to avoid jail or death. Though Pavlovich had little first-hand experience with drug cartels, he was well acquainted with their ferocity. In a violent society with many hired guns, the cartel would find and employ elite artisans who thoroughly analyzed situations and developed clean solutions that they executed without emotion or detection—specialists for whom the task of making people vanish was like an oiled, efficient mechanism.

To ensure his payday, Pavlovich needed to track Estrella until he showed the cartel where he was. He turned his car around and drove back to the bus stop, parking inconspicuously across the street. Though his detour to contact the cartel had taken only minutes, Pavlovich breathed his thanks that Estrella remained at the bus stop. When the criminal boarded a bus, Pavlovich followed, stopping discretely behind each stop, checking to see if Estrella got out. Eventually Estrella stepped off and entered a movie theater. Pavlovich bought a ticket and followed him inside. Estrella sat through the movie twice, left the theatre, and boarded a bus. He got off by the same strip mall where Pavlovich had first seen him, and walked to a small, seedy motel nearby. Pavlovich parked in view of Estrella's room. It was getting dark. Pavlovich was an adept and experienced tail and was confident that Estrella had no idea he had been followed.

Pavlovich had spent years doing surveillance duties in the several republics of the former Soviet Union. He disliked the job, but someone had to do it, and KGB was not shy about assigning tasks, even to those of rank, to keep their skills fresh. In this present case, Pavlovich could not afford to hire an assistant, and he didn't trust anyone with this responsibility. A corrupt or incompetent accomplice would jeopardize the money. He wanted all of it. He needed all of it.

Pavlovich watched, deep in thought. He didn't know how many men would come to the airport, but he guessed two would arrive on the flight. He reasoned they were coming from Orlando after researching the area code of the number that appeared on his cell phone when he received his instructions for the meet. He based almost all of his assumptions about espionage and criminal operations upon the stark operations of the former KGB, where he had served his apprenticeship and many journeyman years. Although he congratulated himself for his use of Google in this case, he had not kept up with many other technological advances in spy craft.

These men would be dangerous, not that that worried him; he had dealt with such. He had the scars. Was not his very existence a silent, decisive affirmation that he was in the game?

There was something incongruous about Pavlovich and his occupation, however. His work required a thick skin, but underneath rested a fundamental insecurity about death. He feared the blank, non-existent state that he pictured death being, and couldn't explain why it bothered him so much. His apprehension drove him to a priest years ago who explained that it was not God's original intention that anyone die, that God offered eternal life to those who would receive it. Pavlovich considered these words but with them came paralysis from a reflexive, accusatory sense that God's offer was simply not extended to the likes of him, a man whose God was the state, disqualified because of things he had done or was doing. Pavlovich's need for work held him in a job that he thought was his only calling. He resigned himself to it—a strange, interminable performance that required varying actions in different days that were alike in loneliness, desire, and desperation.

He drank too much. He always had, but as a young man he could hold his liquor. Now, his mind and body simply could not rebound as before. Despite the increasing severity of the penalties for imbibing, he could not stop.

Pavlovich had very nearly wrestled in the Olympics. In ensuing years, much of his prowess had been robbed by beating out a living among the merciless, machinelike corps of the KGB. Brutally long hours and travel forced him to neglect his physical gifts. His impressive muscularity ebbed, leaving behind only his considerable bulk.

Pavlovich favored a thin, black, knee-length leather overcoat that blunted the wind and weather without overheating him. The coldest Pacific Northwest weather was nothing compared to frigid Soviet winters, but the continual grey skies and rain depressed him. Dripping rainwater from roofs and downspouts reminded him of oppressive ghosts from past interrogations.

While surveilling Estrella's motel room from a quiet, nearly vacant parking lot across the street, Pavlovich continued his ruminations on the past and present, and when he grew tired of that, he turned on the radio and found a talk show. His mind was carried from one topic to another, none of which meant a thing to him. It wasn't stimulating, but the noise was better than waiting in silence, which made the clock stop. In Ukraine, he and his comrades often spent uninterrupted hours waiting, watching, and listening in a maddening cacophony of silence, as if they heard each other's thoughts roaring at one another.

Pavlovich spent an endless, monotonous afternoon waiting for Estrella to leave his room. He needed to monitor him until the men from Florida arrived in the morning. He had already ruled out hiring someone to watch Estrella, even during the time Pavlovich went to meet his contacts at the airport, and the Ukrainian considered expanding the window during which he would allow Estrella to go unwatched. Perhaps Estrella would stay inside this evening. Pavlovich was tired and hungry, and he wanted to go home. He hoped that Estrella would stay put.

Pavlovich turned the ignition key but there was no response. After several moments of anger in which he cursed God, he forced himself to calm down. He blamed an aging battery that no longer held a charge; listening to the radio that afternoon hadn't helped.

Using his cell phone, he dialed AAA and gave his location. A half hour later, loud braking and the rapid crackling of an idling diesel jarred him from unusual and unrelated images in the beginning stages of sleep. He popped the hood of his car, got out, and a Latino tow-truck driver led him through the necessary paperwork required to get a jump. Five minutes later, his engine idled smoothly. The AAA employee left and Pavlovich got back in his car. Glancing toward the motel, he noticed Estrella watching him intently from his window. *How long Estrella watching?* He felt his face and neck flush in frustration and embarrassment. *Surveillance skills sink to level of crapper.* Feeling powerless and incompetent, Yevgeny Pavlovich drove home.

He actuated his garage door remote at a predetermined location he formulated through meticulous testing. The remote's effectual range was .27 kilometers from his residence. At that distance he found an easily recognizable landmark, a white plastic mailbox, and used it as a marker. For security reasons, he waited precisely 3 seconds after passing the mailbox at 25 mph before pressing the button.

Immediately undertake initiation of cooking. Appetite is presently very strong. TV dinners, though poor eating quality, are adequate tonight. He pulled two from the freezer, took them from their cardboard containers, and, meticulously following the instructions, punctured the clear plastic coverings only above the raspberry cobbler. He placed the dinners in the microwave and started the timer.

Pavlovich went back to the garage and retrieved his battery charger from a cabinet. He hooked it up to his car and walked back into the kitchen just in time to hear the microwave signal that his food was ready. He set them on a TV tray and seated himself on the ottoman. As he ate the tasteless food, he watched *The Bourne Ultimatum* in Ukrainian. The synchronization of the actors' lips with the Ukrainian dialogue was imprecise because the actors had spoken English during filming. As he watched, he drank often from a bottle of vodka, and was carried along more and more by the action and pathos. By the end of the movie, and as he had concluded after other viewings of the *Bourne* serial, he had a strong hunch that Jason Bourne carried Ukrainian blood.

He arose on the morrow and dressed, too hung over to eat. Running late, he did not even stop to brew coffee, a deeply ingrained habit that only the peril of lost mammon could nullify. He went out the door of the kitchen to the garage, removed the battery charger, and got into the Cadillac. After opening the garage door with the remote, he pulled out and watched as the door closed to insure that no one ran inside at the last moment.

At the airport he parked and put the receipt marking his entry time on the dashboard, forgetting his gun in the glove box as he focused on arriving to the meet on time. He walked across the sky bridge to the terminal. He was almost to the concourse when the throbbing beat of his phone jarred him. He answered it and heard the same male voice who called the day before, though from a different phone number. Pavlovich noted that the new number was, disturbingly, from a local area code.

"Do not speak. Listen. There has been a change. Go to the Horizon counter and purchase a roundtrip ticket to Portland. The shuttle leaves every hour. Get on the one leaving in 20 minutes. When you get to Portland, do not go out through security. Wait in the secure part of the airport. I will call again. If you understand these instructions, hang up." Waiting only a moment, in which his poverty painfully but quickly overrode his rising doubts, Pavlovich hung up.

Although his face remained expressionless, inside he was crushed and angry. *Unbelievable!* Remembering his forgotten handgun, he allowed that at least he would not have to return it to his car before leaving on the shuttle. That would ensure that he had enough time to buy his ticket and pass through security.

He made his way to the Horizon desk, where he paid $200 for a flight that would have cost less had it not been so immediate. He used his credit card, which was nearly maxed out. There was no helping it. If he wanted the big payout, he would have to invest. He could only hope that he would be reimbursed.

As he rode the underground train to the gate, he wondered if he should have hired help. He had quickly assumed, without thinking matters through as his former bosses forced him to do, that he could handle the job himself, and that he would not have to share any of the 100 grand. He tried to steady himself, thinking that the man he was to meet would have just gotten off a plane, so wouldn't have a weapon. Normally though, he would have brought help in dealing with men he knew nothing about. He would especially have done so in the perilous districts of Moscow and St. Petersburg, and probably in the republics as well. And he had been young then.

Da, Pavlovich is player and these men will not be wise to take lightly. Referring to himself in the third person increased his confidence, helping him to consider himself from an external, impartial perspective. He surveyed his life and saw a man who worked out at the gym twice a week until he sweated. Surely that was worth something. He was perhaps one of the older men at the gym, sitting there on the bench with a dumbbell working his arms as he studied the pictures and captions of *People* and *Us* magazines. It was true that he did not practice marksmanship much, but he researched martial arts on the Internet.

When he touched down in Portland, he did not pass through security, but sat and waited for a call, as instructed. He kept expecting to hear the ringtone that would alleviate his anxiety, and even imagined that his phone rang for a moment at one point, though it had not. Thirty minutes passed, and then an hour. Another disappointment, a feeling he was becoming more familiar with as he aged. He had a setback, and then something even more dismaying happened. His condition after the first letdown shone in its relative lightness compared with how he felt after the second. Plans collapsed, expectations were deferred or vanished altogether.

Twenty more minutes crawled by. He cycled through feelings of anger, fear of loss, paranoia, and boredom. Worse, his bargaining chips with the cartel were diminishing by the minute. What if Estrella left his motel?

Too frustrated to sit any longer, he stood up and walked to a coffee shop. He wolfed down an expensive sweet roll and started on a coffee, but could barely swallow the acidic, lukewarm swill. It reminded him of Czech or even Polish coffee. He threw the nearly full cup in a trash can and left the shop without clearing his table. A Starbucks drew him magnetically. He anticipated the pleasing hot coffee, upscale setting, and music. It would afford him a break from his frustrating and unproductive morning. It was just then that the insistent ringtone of his phone violated his reverie with uncomfortable thoughts of cartel hoods and his penury. He growled a harsh *da* into the receiver, realizing that for the first time in months he had lapsed into his native tongue. Just apparent through his riling haze of irritation and distress, he perceived that he was being played.

From the tiny speaker of the phone a voice with no accent or emotion implored, "Return to Seattle now. Your contact awaits you. After your arrival you will find him reading a newspaper by the Horizon desk in the secure satellite terminal."

My God. Back to Seattle. Contact waits for me*!*

Pavlovich scanned the overhead monitor and saw that the next Horizon flight to Seattle left in 10 minutes. He hurried to his gate, gave the ticket to the gatekeeper, and entered the small turboprop. Fifty fretful minutes later he deplaned and stalked up the Jetway to the SeaTac terminal, ruminating over how poorly his day had gone. It was after noon, and he was tired, frustrated, and disoriented. Except for the small pastry, he had not eaten or had a legitimate coffee. His car was racking up an expensive parking tab, and he had just paid for a useless flight to Portland. He had not yet met his contact, likely a dangerous man with whom he was to do a risky, undefined task while alone and unarmed. No one, except potential enemies, knew where he was. It was possible that he had been observed, or tailed, and had not even thought to watch for it, again forgetting the training instilled in him from his earliest years at KGB. He cursed himself for becoming lazy and careless.

A thought crept into Pavlovich's frantic mind: He could still call Sergey, though he knew that his cartel contact might be close by, and he didn't want to risk being on the phone when they met. He stopped and retrieved his phone. Sergey had a gun and his spy craft was passable. Grasping for any kind of help, the Ukrainian dialed Sergey and waited as the phone rang. No one answered, and he could not leave a message because the mailbox was full. Sergey eluded people by keeping it full. Pavlovich hoped his friend would see he had called.

As he emerged from the Jetway, he saw a seated man reading a newspaper by the Horizon desk. There was no mistaking him, as there were no other people in the area. The man sat in a row of low slung, wide, black, imitation leather seats, with chrome legs and armrests.

"Do you know where Pioneer Square is?" the man asked with a hint of Spanish accent. His demeanor was relaxed, his eyes lively.

"On southern part of downtown," Pavlovich mumbled as though his mouth were full of marbles. "I think sun shines this afternoon, maybe 2:30," Pavlovich said, initiating the second set of passphrases.

"That will be good for sightseeing," the man said. He noted the Ukrainian's rough pronunciation and phrasing, but Pavlovich had passed the test. Without warning he rose from his seat and began to walk toward baggage claim. Surprised, Pavlovich had no alternative but to follow. He didn't know how long the man had been waiting. As they moved away from the Horizon desk, they passed the open door of a bar serving hard liquor. Pavlovich saw two men stand, leave the bar, and follow them. The man with the Spanish accent didn't glance backwards. He reached a narrow escalator, stepped aboard, and began to descend. Pavlovich filed in behind. When he looked back, the two men were on the escalator about 15 feet behind them and avoided glancing at him.

Something wrong. He didn't know who these men were or where they had come from. He began doubting that the number with the Orlando area code he'd seen was actually dialed in Orlando. The call could come from anywhere in the world, including Seattle.

Perhaps the call had come from someone sitting in a car across the street from his house while they researched his background.

Among spies and criminals, a critical difference between professionals and novices was their use of resources and their willingness to spend money. Professionals left little to chance and spent significantly to minimize risks.

Pavlovich silently berated himself for walking into this situation alone. Flying insects buzzed inside his stomach. He tried to convince himself that his fears were unfounded by recalling war stories he'd survived, but was overridden by the guilt that he had acted against his training and long experience. Wisdom was supposed to come with age; instead he'd become careless and desperate. His quick, easy way to make money was disintegrating. He had been drawn in. He thought of his morning, flying to Portland, waiting, coming back, all to insure he was alone, unarmed, and unnerved. Now he was outnumbered too. A chill worked along the back of his neck. He would do well to survive, let alone make any money.

As he and the other man got off the escalator and walked several paces toward the doors of the underground transit linking back to the main terminal, the others quickened their steps and slipped in closely behind. This did not surprise Pavlovich. They stood together waiting for the next coach. Pavlovich looked around, wondering if they would try anything here. Escalators fed a continual stream of passengers to this large waiting room, the only exit from the satellite terminal. *They don't do anything now.*

The stranger who had been reading the newspaper suddenly and unexpectedly turned: "Good morning, friend." Pavlovich supposed that the most bizarre things are those that might seem commonplace under different circumstances. He had expected that he was to follow the man without letting on that they knew each other.

"Good morning," replied Pavlovich cautiously, his accent and slow pronunciation contrasting with the man's clipped greeting. *Why talk to me here?*

"*Mene zvut' Saĭmon Ramires,*" the well-dressed man said, his eyes glittering. Pavlovich tried to appear unfazed: the man had just introduced himself in Russian as Simone Ramirez.

"And my name is Yuri Andropov," Pavlovich replied, hoping his joke would be acknowledged. It was not.

"You should always tell the truth my friend," Ramirez said. "These gentlemen are Misters Ortega and Hermosa," Ramirez explained, waving toward the men who joined them. Ramirez wanted to make sure Pavlovich knew there were three of them, and not one. Condescendingly treating Pavlovich like a novice, Ramirez had riled the Ukrainian. As they were introduced, neither man looked at Pavlovich. Their calculating eyes continuously darted about their surroundings, like wolves on the steppes. Pavlovich doubted the names were real. The men were the same height and coloring, with similar facial features. They appeared to be brothers. Stocky and fit, they paid little attention to Pavlovich, scanning for anything threatening or suspicious.

An uncomfortable silence followed the introductions. Pavlovich did not know what to expect. They waited for the tram for several minutes. More travelers joined them, also forced to await transportation to the main terminal.

Pavlovich was sure Ramirez was the leader. He was about 40. His dapper cloth raincoat of a rich burgundy color covered an expensive suit. With wire-rimmed glasses and a slender face, he looked like a scholar, and reminded Pavlovich of a schoolteacher he'd had in another life, though his teacher would never be dressed like this. Ramirez had a casual way about him, an economy of movement. *I am fool for not bringing backup*, Pavlovich thought yet again. *Sergey would help me for thousand dollars, only 1 percent of job.*

Ramirez's eyes were the one feature over which he did not have full control: While animated and absorbing, they darted about and conveyed messages counter to Ramirez's words. Pavlovich realized that he had an inward compulsion to submit to what Ramirez wanted, to please him. Ramirez seemed to expect it as a matter of course. The Ukrainian resisted.

The doors of the arriving tram opened. The four men entered and sat, Pavlovich near Ramirez, the "brothers" slightly apart as if they were no longer in the same party. A recorded message announced the next stop and warned them to prepare for movement. The doors shut and the automated vehicle lurched forward.

Pavlovich appeared disinterested, but thoughts raced inside his large, block-like head. He had hoped to drive the men to Estrella in his Cadillac. But that would guarantee his vulnerability, as his hands and attention would be occupied. He hoped he wasn't sweating, which would reveal his alarm.

Upon arrival at the main terminal, Ramirez led them by newsstands, restaurants, and Starbucks, all beckoning to Pavlovich like sirens. The men continued with Pavlovich trapped between them. He tried to steer them toward the down escalator to baggage claim to gain time. He thought about the trick of vaulting from the down escalator to the up, desperate as that was. He was grasping at anything now.

"No, my friend, we have no luggages," Ramirez said flatly.

"All this way and you don't stay?" Pavlovich asked, feigning surprise, his bushy blond and grey eyebrows rising. Ramirez walked on without answering. Stealing a look behind, Pavlovich saw that the brothers followed; they were so similar, with sinewy, hypnotic, disquieting movements. He wondered how many men they had killed.

As Pavlovich acknowledged how they had cleverly ensured he was unarmed, he comforted himself with the thought that at least they also had no weapons; they had met in the secure part of the terminal. There was that. Though outnumbered, he felt he had a prayer against unarmed men.

Twenty steps further Pavlovich saw two more men fall into step with them. Ramirez never even glanced over. A rush of adrenaline made Pavlovich's scalp tingle. He thought things were bad before; now they were horrible.

Trap from start. These newcomers would be armed. They joined the troupe in the insecure part of the airport.

Ramirez paused to let the two newcomers lead. There were now five cartel men walking with Pavlovich through the airport as an entourage. The brothers watched for tails. The assembly exited a door that led to the busy airport thoroughfare where vehicles dropped off people free to fly anywhere they wished.

Pavlovich's stomach clenched and his surroundings became surreal. He was alone, and couldn't communicate his distress to anyone. As the outside environment grew more foreign and antagonistic, he became aware of his body, senses, and thoughts. *Wait. Watch for opportunity, any small advantage.* His situation felt like a competition, and he thought of wrestling.

One level below, arriving passengers grabbed their bags and walked out to the main thoroughfare. Ramirez and his men had no luggage. Again, he saw a strategy in this, a small ploy to foil tails.

The two newcomers led them to a dark maroon, late-model Ford Victoria parked at the curb. A Sky Cap stood guard over it. One of the brothers tipped him a 20-dollar bill, and the porter moved away.

"Please get into the car now Mr. Yevgeny Pavlovich," Ramirez said, using the Ukrainian's full name, though Pavlovich had not divulged it.

"But my car?" Pavlovich protested, stalling. "I pay for parking."

"You can get it later," Ramirez said calmly but forcefully. Pavlovich yearned to sit in his car, if only to escape his present difficulty. He would do well even to see it again.

The men directed him to the right rear of the Ford. After he got in, one of the brothers went around, entered the car, and strapped on his own shoulder harness. The newcomers sat in front. Ramirez evidently wanted the firepower in the same car as Pavlovich. These men had black hair, light jackets, and gloves. The man in the seat next to Pavlovich told him to buckle in and asked him for his cell phone. Moments after relinquishing the phone, it began to ring, but with a different ringtone from his regular disco one. *Sergey! Terrible, terrible timing!* The man turned the phone off without even glancing at the Ukrainian, professional that he was. Ramirez and the other brother hailed a taxi and indicated to the men in the Crown Victoria that they should follow. Once underway, the man who took Pavlovich's phone removed its battery and SIM card and placed them carefully into a small, clear plastic bag.

*   *   *

Pavlovich contemplated why the men would not just allow him to take them to Estrella and give him his money. Perhaps it was because they did not want to be linked to Estrella; if Pavlovich lived, he would be a liability to them. Why had he not considered this before?

Pavlovich stopped scolding himself; it was not helpful. He decided that he had three options: he could go where the men took him without resistance; he could try to overpower the men in the car; or perhaps, if he were lucky, he might be able to jump from the moving vehicle.

While he sat in the back of the Ford with his captors, he objectively, though quickly, considered each of his options.

Going with them was fine until they arrived at their destination. There might be an opportunity there for him to overpower them and escape, but he doubted it, and the longer he waited, the worse his chances. Once at the destination they would begin to torture him.

His only trump card with the first option was a long shot, that by not telling them what they wanted to know he might live. He would stay alive until he disclosed the information they wanted. They would try to find the subtle boundary between his maximum pain threshold and death. Pavlovich found this option unappealing; being made to suffer before eventually giving these men what they wanted and then being killed just wasn't fair. If he had to die, why give them any satisfaction? He considered the second option.

He could fight them in the car as they drove. They would probably overpower him and wound or kill him. If he survived, this option dreadfully resembled the first: They would torture him until he talked. The newcomer who was not driving sat in front with his back against his door, his right hand in his coat; Pavlovich knew what he gripped. He knew he would have to attack there first, leaving himself open to the brother sitting in the back on his left. This man looked strong, and even if he didn't have a weapon, he would hurt Pavlovich. Worse, Pavlovich realized that the driver almost certainly carried a gun also. He could stop the car and shoot, or just turn around and fire while driving; Pavlovich knew all too well that it could be done. His odds with this option were poor, but he liked them better than the first.

He considered jumping from the car. He would surely be hurt, perhaps severely enough to die, but it was better than death by torture, and he wouldn't have to reveal where Estrella was. Still, jumping was not optimal: Whenever traffic forced the car to slow, his captors watched him attentively. Pavlovich figured he would probably not get out of the car before they shot him. They only relaxed their attention slightly once the car was moving. From his perspective, the faster the car was moving when he jumped, the more his chance of not being shot before exiting the car.

Pavlovich had difficulty deciding between the pitiful alternatives. The longer he took making up his mind, the less feasible some options became. The intense pressure hurt his stomach and he realized that his breaths had become short, shallow gasps. He forced himself to breathe more regularly to avoid hyperventilating. Sweat rolled down his neck and his underarms were damp. He couldn't remember ever being in a tighter spot. Death was close.

A call to pray surged into his consciousness. Though praying was not something he had ever considered before, it appealed strongly to him now. *God, are you there? Please help me! It is not fair that these men get this information and kill me too. Don't you think? What should Pavlovich do?* He opened his eyes and looked at his captors, half expecting them to have heard his fervent internal request.

He immediately felt calmer, and then a soft, firm instruction to jump came to him in the same way that impressions and forgotten information appeared in his mind. He recognized that the soft impressions that seemed to come from a different dimension had been God all along. That God would speak to him like this showed that He cared for him. The realization was instantaneous, like an invisible chameleon changing color and becoming visible, or a cocoon opening, or a baby being born.

He was still in the presence of his enemies.

When the brother next to him glanced away for a moment, Pavlovich casually brushed his hand against the buckle of his seatbelt and unfastened it. No one noticed.

When should he jump? *Soon* came the answer. The Crown Vic was in the far right traffic lane, traveling about 50 miles per hour. He slowly leaned forward in his seat and pushed his butt against the seatback. As he did this, he gathered his big legs beneath him. He quickly opened his door handle, pushed the door hard against the wind, and leaped out and away from the moving car. As he wrapped his arms around his head, he had a quick vision of blurred ground. In the instant before smacking the pavement, Pavlovich realized that life was so often a choice of the lesser evil rather than the greater good. It was a pity.

But now he also knew that God cared for him.

Thoughts of Mortality

When I was 12, I attended a weekend campout with my Boy Scout troop to celebrate the centennial of the Gettysburg Address. With fellow scouts and our dads, I camped for a weekend, went on a hike of about ten miles (this distance was too far for a lot of us kids), and then memorized the Gettysburg Address. We recited the address as a group in order to receive our Gettysburg scout medals. As I think about the whole experience, what touched me most was the kindness of the leaders in awarding a medal to every child, even kids like me who couldn't hike ten miles or memorize all of the address. Because I showed up and did my best, I was counted with the successful. I cherished my medal for many years, and I'm sure its preciousness was linked to the generosity of those leaders. It was my first lesson in grace, a foreshadowing of the amazing grace I would receive later in life.

The lines from Lincoln's speech still come strongly to me after all these years: "Now we are engaged in a great civil war, testing whether that nation or a*ny nation* so conceived and so dedicated can long endure."

Our nation has endured because of the great sacrifice of so many, so much spilled blood. Our nation exists today because of the Civil War and Lincoln's heroic leadership, among many other great sacrifices.

There is so much sin now, and in the past. Sin is people missing God's will for their lives, separating themselves from and willfully remaining clueless about God's thoughts and plans for them, when people are hurtful to themselves, and at times, hurtful to others in even greater measure.

I think of Germany during the Nazi years. Led by Hitler and other racist hardliners, the German culture was complicit in committing genocide. So many Germans were completely out of God's will, persecuting and murdering millions of Jews and others. They were terribly off base, as was Japan in their conquest of the East. My nephew's grandfather was one of the survivors of the Bataan Death March, during which as many as 11,000 American and Filipino soldiers were killed by the Japanese on a six-day forced march, from bayoneting, beating, starvation, and exposure. He even survived Japanese imprisonment afterward, and was freed at the end of the war. He was one of the fortunate; of those who surrendered at Bataan, 57 percent died on the March and later during the war. He knew inexpressible cruelty and horror, surviving only by God's grace. The Japanese apologized for the Bataan Death March in 2009. The point here is that as Germany and Japan were during the Second World War, any society or group of people at any time can be fully out of line with God's will. And I, as a human, qualify for being error-prone. We desperately need God's guidance continually.

The Bible says that without the shedding of blood, there is no remission of sins. We know that our Jesus died once for all, that whoever receives Him has their sins forgiven by His blood. And His sacrifice was perfect.

But what of those who have not accepted His sacrifice? Because of God's decree, must a land (or lands as in the case of the World Wars) receive other blood periodically to remain in alignment with God's declaration? Can any nation endure where there is no shedding of blood? (Not that the shedding of any blood other than the Savior's can cleanse sin.)

Maybe God allows some of His saints to be sacrificed so that unbelievers will come to belief. Maybe some people will never believe unless there is blood spilled for or even by them in their lifetimes, pointing back to the perfect sinless blood of the Savior.

Maybe my blood will be required to free someone.

Memoir

I'm a Believer

My dad and sister Carol called from Santa Barbara, California, where my folks lived. They told me that my mom had been taken by ambulance to the hospital, where doctors removed a liter of fluid from her lungs. Besides making it difficult for her to breathe, the fluid had also caused congestive heart failure.

During a second phone conversation with Carol several days later, I could sense her tears as we talked; she wasn't sure Mom would make it, and she sounded shaken. Intertwined with her wavering voice I heard God's firm, gentle request: *Will you go to California for her?* Oddly, He didn't seem to be as concerned for my mother or father as He was for her. After hanging up, I made reservations to fly down from Seattle.

I booked an early morning flight to save 40 bucks, and slept only two hours before taking off. When I bought the ticket, the savings had seemed significant. Between the scant rest and other factors, it turned out to be hard-earned cash.

Mom had recently been transferred from the hospital to the full-care wing of the retirement center where she and Dad stayed before her hospitalization. Carol warned me that she looked very ill.

I arrived in Santa Barbara just before noon and walked out of the small airport. I removed the coat I had been wearing. The climate and vegetation were so different from the Pacific Northwest. Here was warmth for frigid rainfall, clear skies for cloudy, and palm trees for ferns and dark-green conifers.

I missed this place. I had attended and graduated from high school nearby, and lived here for a time after dropping out of college in Los Angeles years ago. It was hard to discern why I missed living here. Certainly the climate made for an easier time, but the feelings I had now after entering this pleasant environment were probably just a temptation to escape the stresses of my life up north, and perhaps tangentially the circumstances of my mother's current sickness, as if moving here would do all that. It never would, of course.

Dad and Carol were waiting for me in the temporary parking area in front of the airport in Dad's pristine, white '93 Lincoln Continental. He got out of the car and walked gingerly toward me, toting his portable oxygen supply. He smiled and offered his hand, which I took, and then I hugged him. Mildly embarrassed, he opened the gigantic trunk for me to deposit my rolling travel bag. The cavernous space, though half full of golf clubs and various neatly arranged surplus items, absorbed it easily. He pulled the lid to within a few inches of closing and released it. The trunk mechanism engaged, slowly pulling the lid tight. He loved this feature of his car. More than once he told me not to slam the trunk: Just bring the lid close and the car would do the rest. My Dad was a former aeronautical engineer. Whether it pertained to car mechanics, electronics, or clock repair—all of which had been hobbies and that he had been good at—his motto was *Don't force anything*.

As Dad slowly paced back to the driver's seat, I walked to the car's rear side door. I heaved it open and settled into the plush and roomy white leather passenger seat, the feel of it evoking pleasant memories from my time in California. I found the seat much nicer than my accommodations on the plane, with considerably more legroom. Dad drove to his retirement home, and for a moment I rested, watching the agreeable Southern California countryside roll by through the tinted glass.

But despite the Lincoln's elegance, size, and weight, Dad drove it like a stock car, vigorously applying the throttle and brake in turn. The car got poor mileage, but he couldn't care less about that. He followed traffic on the freeway at a car's length. Between jabs at my imaginary brake, it occurred to me how exhausted and scattered I was. My tank was empty, *con nada*. A smattering of Spanish was coming back as I noticed its abundant use everywhere, as it usually did when I visited Santa Barbara.

We arrived at my parents' retirement home and Dad parked his Lincoln, the generous boundaries the white lines allotted barely containing its mass. It was better to have empty parking stalls on either side so the car's long, heavy side doors didn't damage adjacent smaller, modern cars.

The facility's name was Valle Placentera (my mother had always referred to it as "the home"). Spanish-style bungalows stood in circular arrangements surrounded by finely manicured lawns and gardens filled with warm-weather succulents and other local subtropical greenery. The elderly inhabitants of Valle Placentera were friendly and kind, and took an interest in the young man (I was in my 60s) from up north. Residents who needed more care, like my mother now, lived in group quarters in the center of the site, named the Health Center.

She had had a difficult time adjusting to the rhythms of retirement living, with its communal evening meal, relatively small quarters, and other rest-home constraints after living in spacious homes with my father for six decades. The Health Center was a much more constricting environment, one that made her previous living arrangement at Valle Placentera seem like the places she had lived with Dad before they moved to the home.

The door to the Health Center stood between other buildings, the entrance set back from the main walkway in a kind of tropical Southern California garden cloistered by other parts of the campus. Thick, long stalks of grass grew profusely and surrounded a miniature pond. Frogs hidden in the long grass called to one another as we walked by. The exotic sound was charming, but also added to the disorientation brought about by sleep deprivation, air travel, and the significant change in weather.

I barely recognized the woman in Mom's room. Her head was tilted back on the pillow of her inclined bed, eyes closed, mouth agape. She labored to draw air and exhaled in shallow gasps. She appeared to weigh about 80 pounds.

In my early full-gospel days, I never would have said that a person had a disease. Declaring ownership of something negative was not good faith confession, and could hinder someone's healing. One didn't quite accept that a disease was real. It was an illusion created by Satan to fool everyone, especially the person who was ill.

I didn't have the energy for that faith stance now, and hadn't for some years. In the last several months, Mom had contracted scleroderma, a connective tissue disease. Scleroderma had attacked Mom's lung, causing her recent hospitalization. Mom's hands were distorted and she could hardly move them. The disease stretched her skin tightly across the back of her hands and knuckles, hindering her circulation. Her hands felt like cool, hard wax when I held them. I saw how much trouble she had grasping buttons on her sweater, and even holding a spoon. Additionally, scleroderma attacked her esophagus, making it difficult for her to swallow.

Seeing her like this, I accepted that Mom had scleroderma. It was real.

My sister woke Mom and after looking at me, recognition flickered in her eyes, but after a minute she fell back into a deep sleep. Dad woke her a little while later and the same thing happened. Without interacting with her, carrying my tiredness like a troublesome, unconscious acquaintance, my goal was simply to make it through each successive minute, waiting for the end of the day, whenever that would come.

The relentless and wearying moments that held my family and me captive crawled along. Each thing that I did required effort: *think of a question; consider of whom to ask it; find meaning in the answer; persevere, or let it go*? I waited for someone else to say something, and then answered, if directed to me. Mostly we sat silently. When anyone came into the room, it provided a welcome, if momentary, diversion.

There was another room occupant, an elderly woman watching TV from her bed. A curtain divided the room. I tried to resist the TV but the lure of *The Price Is Right*—pretty models, raucous crowd, merchandise—called to me like a siren and I looked. *No way does that car cost that much.* Realizing that I was being drawn in to the aimless show, I forced myself not to listen. This required considerable effort. My resistance waned and my eyes returned, whereupon I looked away again. This cycle repeated itself, a string of small failures.

While our small nuclear family sat among the heavy moments that fell like a kind of troubling rain, my thoughts drifted more than once to my younger sister Nan. She was a nurse practitioner who lived with her family in Missoula, Montana. I missed her strength. It was her and her husband's turn to come see Mom and Dad the next week after Carol and I left. We siblings tried to stagger out visits to give Mom and Dad the best coverage. Nan and Carol, who worked for a hospice group in the Bay Area, applied their fields of expertise lovingly to our mother.

The physical therapist came in and wanted to get Mom up. It took a minute to register. *This is all wrong. You'll hurt her and she might die.*

But I came to see that this was characteristic of this worker, a proactive, gentle woman pushing to keep people alive. Her name was Julienne, "like the beans," she said. God gifted her to be herself, and just as she was and instilled deeply, she loved and helped people.

With Julienne's gentle coaxing and physical support, Mom awoke, stood with Julienne's help, and sat in a wheelchair. Julienne had Mom do as much of the work as she could. Then Julienne led us to a wing of the facility as I followed behind Mom's wheelchair. She helped Mom stand. "Let's walk," she said cheerfully as she fixed a gait belt around my mother's waist. These belts are usually made of cotton and help to steady people as they move. Mom stood and carefully began to walk, Julienne beside her with a firm grip on the belt at the small of her back. Mom revived. She started to talk.

"Why don't you walk with your mother?" Julienne asked with a bright smile, surprising me. I wasn't sure I was capable.

She showed me how to pull up gently on the gait belt in back like she had been doing (I knew I had to hold fast if mom stumbled). Tentatively I assumed the new role, though I grasped the belt with authority in fear of Mom getting hurt. Quickly, my confidence grew. Julienne suggested we might even go outside, but the cool and rainy weather had followed me to Southern California, and she changed her mind.

I looked to the end of the hall and saw Dad staring at us with his mouth agape. He had just spent a grueling week in a confined hospital space with his daughter, waiting on his critically ill wife. Now she was fully conscious, walking and talking with his son. Before this moment he may have thought he would never again see her as she was now.

Sleep-deprivation helped make me more simple and juvenile, and I was aware of God's gentle, positive spirit. Watching Mom recover before my eyes, I hoped expectantly that God's glory and presence would also be obvious and wonderful to everyone else.

It was time to take Mom back and get her ready for lunch. Because of her improvement, she was to eat in the dining room for the first time since returning from the hospital.

We went to her room and then accompanied her to the cafeteria with Dad and Carol. Dad sat beside her at the table. For the first time in a week and a half, Mom fed herself at lunch, albeit slowly, grasping the spoon with her compromised hand.

My sister and I took the opportunity to eat in the main dining room. We were not allowed to sit with Mom and the intensive care patients, though they had made an exception for Dad. We were hungry, and happy to allow my parents some time to themselves. While pleased with Mom's significant progress, I was exhausted. I had coasted along on joy, but now that we weren't in Mom's presence I needed help. After a lunch of *Camarones a la Diabla*, I felt more energetic, but as the afternoon progressed, so did an intense headache behind my eyes.

Julienne had been God's agent that day. As she was getting ready to leave work for the day, I walked to her, grasped her hand, looked in her eyes, and said, "I like you and am so glad you're taking care of my mother." This uncharacteristic burst of affection and affirmation rose up spontaneously from my pleasure at Mom's recovery. Tears appeared in Julienne's eyes and she hurried away before breaking down completely. There was a temptation to think that I shouldn't have said what I did because it made Julienne cry, but I think it needed saying. Maybe it was days like this that kept her going. I imagined her job was difficult, as she watched many patients that she truly loved decline and die. I pictured the enemy suggesting to her that her labor of love was in vain, but I was sure it was not. It undoubtedly made all the difference at times.

Revenge of the Sith

The Sith entered the *Star Wars* saga and our lives in 2005, in episode three of the (prequel) trilogy. I wrote an essay decrying what I perceived as Asian facial characteristics of the Sith (who were particularly underhanded and hostile heavies) but no one, including a prominent Christian magazine I approached with a review of the movie, paid any attention. Perhaps I was just seeing things. Apparently, the Sith were not Asian, and did not look Asian, as it turns out, I guess.

In *this* story the Sith represent demons who, because God had so marvelously healed my mother, turned their attention to the interloper from Seattle. My wife rallied many friends and family members to pray for Mom while I was in Santa Barbara, so I can't take any credit for her improvement. At this juncture, the Sith made their appearance as *Camarones a la Diabla*.

At a certain point during the long afternoon, after Julienne left, I apologized to my family members, and told them I had to lie down for a while and went to my room. I set my alarm for an hour because I didn't want to sleep late into the evening.

It was very difficult to get up. I felt worse than before my nap and my stomach was queasy. In my uninhibited eating at lunch, aggravated by lack of sleep and having not eaten much previously during the day, I had eaten the abundant shrimp and spices in *Camarones a la Diabla*, a delicacy of the upscale cafeteria at Valle Placentera. I usually don't eat shrimp because of problems they had caused me in the past.

I went to the ward anyway and met my family. After a time an aide wheeled my mother into the special cafeteria in the facility and Carol, Dad, and I went to the regular dining room, where over 100 retirement center residents had turned out for the evening meal.

There was great pressure to eat and be sociable but I felt miserable. After eating a few soda crackers I excused myself and tried to walk off my malaise outside. The longer I walked, the worse I felt. Time passed very slowly. I prayed fervently: *God don't let this happen, not now, on this trip. It's important for me to have my health to help out while I'm here, not need care myself.* I went back to my room and threw up three times over what seemed like an interminable time.

I knew of no circumstance when I felt further from God than when nauseous and vomiting, prayers for relief not answered, wanting to die. I saw vestiges of pink *Camarones a la Diabla* floating around the toilet bowl on several occasions. Thoughts of feeling bad the whole time I was in Santa Barbara vexed me. I was absolutely devastated.

The Sith *had* their revenge. But by the next day I could almost eat normally, and the Sith had to invent other devices to attack me, which they did, as usual; catch as catch can.

The Days Pass

Our days were filled with keeping Mom company, individually or together. When Dad grew tired, Carol or I would take the next shift. It was a monotonous, enclosed existence.

Paul

I became acquainted with many of the residents in the Health Center at the retirement home. I first noticed Paul, who, amidst a challenging environment that seemingly discouraged tidiness, remained well groomed and dignified. Paul did not (or could not) speak, however, and it was anyone's guess where his mind was. Paul stared at or looked away from those who tried talking with him, showing no hint of comprehension or a desire to communicate. Still, he had a mild, even friendly air about him. Like almost everyone else in this division of the facility, Paul was in a wheelchair.

Each Friday a different musician came and played for the residents at the Health Center. While I was there, Heinz, an aged but lively German accordionist, gave a concert in a relatively large hospital room to 15 elderly patients, many of whom draped blankets over their wheelchairs to stay warm. Heinz specialized in well-known show tunes and classics that his audience had no trouble recalling. He had an impressive repertoire at his disposal, and on this day "Singin' in the Rain," "Pennies from Heaven," and others of that kind proved popular because of the weather. He also played tunes like "You Are My Sunshine" and "On a Bicycle Built for Two."

Heinz was an enthusiastic entertainer, gently and persistently encouraging his audience to participate by singing, clapping, and, for the one who still could, dancing at times. I looked over at Paul and saw that he was keeping time with his leg under his blanket, a surprising display of cognizance.

During "Home on the Range," Paul suddenly broke into an almost operatic performance of the song. On key and in time with the accordionist, as though comfortably alone onstage in front of hundreds, he continued full-voice through the finale. Heinz immediately swung from lead entertainer to the subordinate role of accompanist, as if he had anticipated something like this.

Dad grabbed my shoulder and gazed at Paul. "He never talks!" he whispered, perhaps a bit louder than he had intended. God was in the house.

The next day Mom and I sat in the TV viewing area watching a black-and-white film. That TV perpetually showed American Movie Classics. The morning's offering was *Come and Get It*, made in 1936, with Edward Arnold, Frances Farmer, Walter Brennan, and Joel McCrea. I never quite understood the title. The movie was about logging and the vicissitudes of a family and their friends, some of whom got rich while others didn't, and some died. The main character knew he had made mistakes, but tried to make the best of them, and became successful, but he wasn't half so lucky in love. Two women played him for a fool at different times.

Paul was among seven people in the room, and despite occasional lapses, he made a decent effort at keeping his eyes open and focused toward the screen. (Others were not doing as well with the screening.) As was typical with him, he wore his grey hair combed nicely back from his face, and he dressed in clean, fashionable clothes. I waved to him and he pointedly looked the other way.

After a time, I got a strong impulse to tell Paul that Jesus loved him. I recalled past experiences when I had done this with people; these hadn't always gone well so I tried to ignore the prompting. My impulse to tell him about God's love challenged my reticence.

A Filipino aide with a kindly face and gentle manner came to take Paul to lunch. Paul asked the young man urgently, "Are you a Christian?" It was as if the same spirit that had prompted me to communicate my faith also fell on Paul.

"Yes I am," replied the aide simply.

"So am I," Paul said.

"You are my brother then," the aide responded softly with his clipped accent.

Their exchange was not typical of what I had seen in the Health Center because of the emotion the conversationalists invested in the dialog, which was belied by the casual and quiet manner of their speaking.

I was surprised by Paul's pointed, intelligent conversation, but I set these feelings aside because I felt something more important was happening. Emboldened and reassured by what I had just seen, and feeling a bit guilty for not moving in faith earlier, I walked to Paul, put my hand on his shoulder, and looked in his eyes. I told him Jesus loved him. His face went through several dramatic changes and then he said in an unexpected mix of resignation and grateful acknowledgement, as if I had somehow just gotten the upper hand on him, "I know." I found out from his wife not long before I returned to Seattle that he had been a pastor for 30 years. I had sensed God's spirit in him.

Life Goes On

After Mom's vast improvement during my first day in Santa Barbara, God continued to work His miracles. But these blessings came amidst the continuing challenges of Mom's memory loss and dementia, her difficulty moving and eating, and her agonizing acceptance that she might not ever return to the bungalow at the retirement center she once shared with Dad. Julienne and the staff were unbelievably loving and supportive. I thanked God for them, and encouraged them however I could. I also thanked God for my sisters and especially for Dad, as he continually supported Mom and spent most of his time in the ward with her.

You Were Meant To Be Here

My last day in Santa Barbara was a Sunday. I woke up to a cloudless sky, a pleasant change from the uncharacteristic rainy and cold weather from the previous four days. Though a little chilly, it was a beautiful, sunny day.

I had been in the ward with my mother for most of that week, and was looking forward to attending church. Since Mom moved into Valle Placentera three years ago, she and I had gone to the service at the retirement home whenever I was in town. Dad didn't go.

I usually enjoyed going to church in the ornate and carpeted multipurpose room of "The Grove" at Valle Placentera when I was in Santa Barbara, though I was usually the youngest person in the congregation by quite a few years. I was engaged in the service among churchgoers of advanced years. Because God's presence was there, He encouraged me, and I believe a child would have been just as engaged because of God's ability to reach multiple generations simultaneously. In one sermon, the pastor explained that God was nowhere near done with people after they moved into a retirement center, that He still had important things for them to do. I found this very helpful personally, because even at 61 I couldn't do as much or be as active as earlier in my life. It reminded me that God does not put people on the shelf at any age, that because of the life He infuses in each of His children, they are included in and symbiotic with the other members of His body. Seeing fellow believers I had met at the communal dinner gave me joy, and the songs spoke of God's presence among us. Even people who are strangers, if they know God, quickly become closer because of His spirit.

I know I shouldn't judge things by my feelings, but that particular morning's service did not feel very inspirational. I was hoping God would show up in some perceptible way, but if He did, I didn't notice. Coming into the room where the service was to be held that morning, I felt led to sit in the first row, and believed that God was making our presence known "in the house."

Mom seemed startled by the pastor's loud singing as he led the hymns, and then she didn't even try to sing. Maybe she didn't know the words. She followed most of his sermon, but flagged at about the three-quarters mark. Her head dropped to her chest. I took her hand as she dozed off. After sitting with her as she slept for what seemed like forever because of my preoccupation with what other people might think of her for sleeping during church, she awoke almost exactly as the pastor uttered his last sentence. All of this came after I had felt inspired to share a public prayer request, delivered with great zeal and faith, that Mom could move higher in the facility's care stages from "Health Center" (where she was now, needing the most care) to "The Grove" (where residents can generally feed themselves and get by with less assistance). The pastor seemed a little surprised at my request, but said publicly, "And of course we'd love to have your mother move to The Grove." Subtly by his tone, he seemed to suggest that this was unlikely. In short, church did not give me the help it often does. That happens occasionally, but I sure could have used a boost that weekend.

With the break from the rain and cold, housebound residents of Santa Barbara poured to the beaches *en masse*, eager to reclaim justification for the sky-high rents and mortgages famous in this town. Every single parking space at Hendry's Beach was taken, including the ample overflow area, so I headed to the beach downtown. After finally finding a spot, I laboriously folded my dollar bills so they would fit into the self-serve parking slots.

I walked along the greenway that fronted sandy Ledbetter Beach. Something about the varied assortment of people and groups enjoying their day at the beach inspired me: Laid-back college kids tossing bean bags, their peers draped over picnic tables cheering and laughing as events unfolded; a troupe of paddleboard surfers gearing up to hit the waves; familial gatherings; and then the last patch of people by themselves at the end of the strip, a group of transients—five men and two women, the men with old stained clothes, long hair, beards, the women of early middle age, dressed hip, seemingly out of place among the others. The women moved about, smoking. One took a hand-rolled cigarette from one of the men. I wondered if it was pot or tobacco. There was no way to distinguish without going closer. I didn't for two reasons: I didn't *want* to know, and for fear of being asked for cash.

A casually dressed man of about 60 stood facing the group, a guitar slung over his shoulder. The sound of the instrument's beautiful open-chord notes and the man's clear, strong voice beckoned me toward the unfamiliar and tough-looking group. His song was enticingly familiar, but I couldn't place it. Although I didn't know it at the time, I now recognize that its haunting tones had deeply affected me in another life, the "me" of an earlier time who felt like a younger brother. I was and wasn't that person anymore, though he held a great interest for me now, as though maybe the way he used to live and act could strengthen or guide me now.

"Whatever was done is done, I just can't recall... It doesn't matter at all..."

The man with the guitar was very talented. He played cleanly, the rhythm carrying the crisp, understated imagery of the song's words home to my heart. I wondered if he were famous; he was that good.

"You see it's all clear... You were meant to be here...

"From the beginning." Da da da da; bomp, bomp bomp.

I felt the Holy Spirit confirm the truth of the words in my gut. All these people at the beach, me, my trip to California to see and help Mom in some way: It was all God's plan. He made the world to be inhabited, by people, by us. He doesn't dislike and isn't bothered by people (like I am). He yearns for a relationship with each one, even, and sometimes especially, the unattractive, like the transients I'd just avoided, and other people whom most people shunned. God was with us, reaching out to us. I felt Him then. Sometimes when I felt Him, tears followed.

I left the group and walked along the beach. I had great peace and no longer felt like I was alone. To my surprise, the singer walked away from the group, leaving his guitar behind. Apparently it belonged to someone else, and he wasn't part of that group. He joined a little girl and a woman dressed in a long, hippies-era flowered skirt, and walked with them in my direction.

I slowed my pace and angled toward them. When I drew near, I said to the guitarist, "That was a great song. I recognized it, but I can't remember the name."

"Emerson, Lake, and Palmer. 'From the Beginning.'"

Ah. My mind worked quickly. "Was that about 1972?"

"Yes."

"You're really good. I love those open-voiced chords. Are you a rock star?"

"No." We continued walking in silence for a moment, and then parted.

I walked and ran for a bit along the gorgeous beach, watching the paddleboard surfers and others in the waves. After a while I went back to the ward and stayed with Mom for a bit longer before going to the airport. My time at the beach had really helped dissipate the confinement of the ward. I wished Mom could have gone with me that day. I was sorry that she had to live in the Health Center. I thought of how happy and vibrant she was earlier in her life, and of the change that had crept in over the years. Now it had come to this. It was heavy and there was no relief.

I flew back to Seattle. Mom continued in her confinement with her life mate by her side until her release in the spring of 2011.

We often walk through hard places in this "valley of tears," and I'm so thankful that there is Someone with us.

When you pass through the waters, I will be with you;
And through the rivers, they shall not overflow you.
When you walk through fire, you shall not be burned,
Nor shall the flame scorch you.

Isaiah 43:2

Short story

The Child King

Now Elisha had become sick with the illness of which he would die.

2 Kings 13:14

For they persecute the ones You have struck,
And talk of the grief of those You have wounded.

Psalm 69:26

There was in ancient times a king, a good and righteous man, who feared God and walked in His ways. He defended his homeland and, unlike his brother and the timid leaders of his brother's realm, always rode at the front of his army. From his youth he defended his people against their enemies.

It was during one such campaign that he was sorely wounded on the battlefield. While the king's army was victorious, he was carried home near death.

"My father, my father," called his son, the only heir to the throne, "you inquired of the priests before you went to battle, and they told you to go. Why are you now wounded?"

"Perhaps it is time for me to be with God, dear boy. God's ways are beyond our understanding, and no one is His counselor."

And so the king died. The common people gathered at his funeral. They prayed that his heir would be as good and great as his father, fearing God and walking in His ways, and God anticipated and heard the prayers of the people.

Child King

The king's son had a friend named James, the only son of a temple priest. James and the king's son played often together and were inseparable.

After the king's funeral, the king's court, priests, and subjects, wealthy and poor, gathered for the heir's coronation. From that day, the heir was called the Child King. He began his reign at the age of 11.

Coronation day was like no other, filled with the blessings and presence of God. As his eyes met those of his friend James across the room, the Child King released his resentment against God for taking his father, opened his heart fully to Him, and accepted that his coronation was God's will. As he recited the vows administered by the high priest, it was not an empty formality: The Child King agreed to honor God, seek the greatest welfare of his people, and to protect them at all costs, so help him God. He promised these things from an undivided heart.

A grievous wrong

As the years passed, the Child King grew in body and spirit, in gentleness, strength, and wisdom, walking in favor with God and humankind. As his father had done, he went to battle against the enemies of his people, always leading his army from the front.

The king married and had children. James became a temple priest like his father. God's hand was with him and He raised him to the office of prophet. In time, because of their increased responsibilities and differing duties, the times of fellowship enjoyed by the Child King and his friend James ended, though James regularly advised the Child King on various matters. On occasions of state when the king saw James seated across the room, he was thankful for the close friendship of their youth.

One day the king rode with Haderach, the mighty and loyal leader of his army, and other men of the king's traveling guard. They came upon a group of frantic peasants and others in a field.

"Go and find out the nature of their trouble and return to me," the king instructed Haderach, who departed promptly.

When he had come back, Haderach told the king: "A tower the peasants were erecting for a nobleman named Cargill fell and crushed a peasant woman who was ministering to her husband as he worked. Her injuries are severe. She can't last long." The king immediately rode to the group of peasants who surrounded the woman. When he got close, he saw that the woman was raving. He dismounted and rushed to her side.

"I recognize you, great king, though now you are no longer a child, as at your coronation," the woman moaned. "As I am near the gates of paradise where I will behold my Lord, I am emboldened to speak from the bitterness of my soul. My husband's and my only daughter has been taken by the nobleman Cargill to raise as his own. Cargill has forbidden us to speak of the matter on pain of my daughter's death, for he said to me, 'If I don't have her, none will.'

"But now near death I find courage to believe in the goodness and power of God and His servant the king to right this wrong. Swear to me now before I die that you will return our dear child to her father and my family."

Greatly moved the king answered, "I will." And so the peasant woman died. As he mounted his horse, the king heard a peasant exclaim to his fellow: "The woman was so troubled about her daughter that she may have prayed for the tower to fall upon her! At least now she has peace, for her face in death looks like the face of an angel of God."

"Are you ready to continue, my king?" Haderach asked.

"No. We go at once to Cargill," said the king, and with that he wheeled his horse and sped to the nobleman's castle. His men had no choice but to follow. And so the child was reunited with her father and the peasant woman's family according to her dying wish.

But that day the Child King gained a mortal enemy in Cargill, a man of vast wealth and power, and of an angry and twisted spirit.

Trial

One day the king noticed scaly patches on his arm below the shoulder. He did not mention the matter.

As time passed and the condition spread, it became increasingly difficult to hide the disease with his vestments. He consulted the physician, but despite the doctor's ministrations, the disease spread until it could no longer be hidden. Eventually, though his wife furiously resisted, the king moved to a separate house for fear of spreading the illness to his family.

The Child King attended to duties of state by day, and then withdrew to his quarters. He lived a lonely existence. He often prayed long into the night for wisdom to lead his people, and he called on God to remove this illness that troubled, weakened, and confused him.

Cargill rises

A day came when the king's court was gathered with the people of the land, and Cargill stood, requesting to be heard. The king gestured with his scepter, indicating that the nobleman could proceed.

Cargill strode uncomfortably close to the king's dais, his purposeful maneuver surprising the audience. He turned and addressed the multitude. "Does it not say in the holy writings that the curse causeless does not come?" He stared hard at the Child King, and then back toward his interlocutors. They murmured assent that it was so.

"And does the Holy Book not say that disease is caused by sin?" Again the crowd allowed that it was so.

Turning toward the king, Cargill shouted, "Then what right does this sinner have to rule over us? Why should I not be king instead?

"Look at him there, propped up on his throne, diseased beyond usefulness, an isolated and futile figure. How can he rule? How could God ever be with such an one?"

The people arose as a single man to defend their king, but Cargill's words cut to their hearts. Scripture backed his reasoning, and because the multitude feared God and were not wise in the spirit of the scriptures, they stood mute and powerless. Until that hour, they believed that their king and God were of one purpose. Cargill's words planted doubt inside their troubled hearts.

The Child King rose from his throne. Though greatly disturbed, he managed to maintain his regal bearing. Did not Cargill's words cut also to his heart, raw and bleeding from nights of unanswered prayer about his condition?

"Court is dismissed," he said sadly, repairing to his separate house. Sleep did not come that night, and on the morrow he did not meet with his court as was his custom. For three days no one saw the king.

The fourth day Haderach, leader of the king's army, loyal and honest man of valor, knocked at the king's door. When he heard no response, he called, fearing that the king might be dead. Loyalty compelled him to wait an interminable period outside. None were permitted to enter these quarters because of the king's decree. He feared returning to court without having seen the king, for that would secure Cargill's ascension to the throne. At long last he heard the king shuffle to the porch.

"Ah, my good Haderach," the king sighed, hoping the loyal guard had come to encourage or support him, or at least to inquire how he was.

"The people are in need of their leader," Haderach said.

The king tried to conceal his disappointment. "Yes, they need a ruler," he agreed.

"Sir, duty compels me to ask, how do you answer Cargill's charges?" The king said nothing. "Sir, please," Haderach implored.

"I have no answer," the king said at last.

"Only say a word rebutting Cargill's accusations and I am with you to the death!" Haderach pleaded.

But the Child King, overcome by the doubts in his own heart and his desire to remain an honest man, could not reply. And so Haderach wistfully departed.

The end of the Child King

In the inward tumult of his frantic heart, the Child King recalled his life, trying to understand what had happened. Had not God been with him? When had He departed?

Certainly not in the early years, when he had been sure that it was God's will for him to be king. And later God brought him a wife and a family. Tears stung his eyes as he remembered their preciousness. Throughout his life God had been with him and delivered him. And then the disease had come.

There seemed to be no defense against God's word as mouthed by Cargill. But was it spoken in God's spirit? Was this accusation truly from God?

He gazed at the knife on the table near his bed in this lonely house where he sequestered himself and his illness. There it was, an instrument of death, lying on the table. He did not imagine turning the dagger on himself, but neither did he resist the notion. Summoning the remainder of his feeble strength, he managed to limp to his pallet and knelt. He called out to God in an agonized sob.

Cargill is right. I am grievously sick, and healing prayers have not changed that. Are You indicating that I am no longer fit to rule? Have I sinned against You, and thus gained this loathsome disease that separates me from family and friend?

O Lord, if Cargill ascends to the throne, it is certain that he will harm this people. How can I allow that? He is greedy and devious. Did You not straitly charge me to protect this people?

I cry out to You with my whole heart. Answer me!

At length the Child King fell asleep, kneeling beside his modest bed.

After a time he was awakened by a touch on his shoulder, and he looked into the kindly eyes of James, his childhood friend, priest, and prophet, who though it was forbidden by decree and fear of contagion, had entered the king's quarters.

"Oh king, I place my hand on your shoulder not as a religious gesture, but as your friend. I am bold to say words to you, and may God not let them fall to the ground.

"He has shown us that He is a God of love, and of friendship. It has been given to you now to know that God is fully with you. Rule this people with His gift of an undivided heart, if in a broken body. This brings God glory, because *His* strength is made perfect in our weakness."

And so the Child King summoned Haderach and vowed that Cargill's charges were unfounded, beginning the deceitful nobleman's demise.

The people followed their king all of his days because they loved him in spite of his disease, and they knew the spirit of God was with him and them.

ॐ ॐ

CPSIA information can be obtained at www.ICGtesting.com
Printed in the USA
BVOW03s2341180314

348054BV00001B/7/P

9 781628 718669